YOU'RE **NOT** DOING IT WRONG

Tools and Truths for When Getting Things Done Feels Hard

Suzy Carbrey

Paperback ISBN: 979-8-9934721-0-2
E-book ISBN: 979-8-9934721-1-9

For the ones who have ever felt like they were "doing it wrong." You never were.

Contents

Introduction

If you are reading this, I'm guessing life might feel a little heavier than it should. Work deadlines keep piling up. Housekeeping slips through the cracks. Relationships require more energy to maintain than you can offer. And underneath it all is that steady hum of shame: *Why can't I just get it together?*

Maybe you have tried the hacks, the perfect planners, the so-called life-changing systems. You start strong, and then, like so many of us, it unravels. You are left thinking you just need more willpower, more discipline, more *something*.

But here is the truth: You do not need to be fixed. You need understanding and support that actually fit the way your brain works.

I know this because I have lived it myself, noticed it in those around me, and worked through it with my clients. I began my career as a speech-language pathologist, helping adults in medical settings rebuild skills like attention, memory, and problem-solving after brain injuries or illnesses. And what I eventually realized is that those same executive functioning skills—focus,

follow-through, planning, getting started, organization, and shifting between tasks—are the same ones
so many of us wrestle with every single day.

That realization is what brought me into ADHD and
executive functioning coaching. Now I work with parents and professionals who feel the constant push and
pull of executive functioning challenges. Many of my
clients, friends, and family are neurodivergent. I even
struggle with my own executive functioning challenges
too, and I use the same strategies I teach every single
day. They do not make life flawless or perfectly consistent. But they work because they make life lighter,
kinder, and more doable.

This book is here to do the same for you.

How to Use This Book

This book was written for real brains—the ones that get
tired, distracted, overwhelmed, or stretched too thin.
You will not find long chapters or complicated systems
here. Each chapter is short, to the point, and meant
to be read in small doses. Think of it as a collection
of tools you can pick up when you need them, not a
manual you have to master all at once.

You do not have to start at the beginning or read in
order. If a chapter title speaks to what you are facing
today, start there. If you only have a few minutes, skip
straight to the end of the chapter, where you will find:

- **Key Takeaways** that capture the heart of the idea

- **Put It into Practice** with simple, doable ways to try it out
- **One Small Action for Future You** to remind you that progress usually starts with one small, kind step

If you do not have the capacity to read the whole chapter, that is okay. The ending sections are designed to give you what you need in a fraction of the time. You can always come back to the chapter later if you want more.

Use this book however works best for you: skim it, dog-ear your favorite parts, jump around, or just read the closing prompts. Bottom line: every approach counts, and it all adds up. You are doing it right.

Closing Note

The goal here is not perfection. It is not about becoming someone who finally has it all together. It is about creating rhythms, systems, and supports that make life lighter and more livable. You will learn to reset your expectations, use tools without guilt, and build momentum one messy, human-sized step at a time.

By the end, I hope you will see what I see in the people I work with every day: you are not broken, and you have always been more resourceful than you realized. With the right supports, you do more than just manage; you create a life that feels lighter, kinder, and more your own.

PART ONE

RETHINKING HOW WE WORK

---

*Setting the stage for a more
compassionate framework*

You're Not Broken, You're Wired Differently

Reframing executive functioning challenges as skill differences—not flaws

———————————————

You are not lazy. You are not broken. You have been trying to live inside systems that were never built with your brain in mind.

That being said, the goal is not to "fix" you but to create a life that fits you—one that works with your wiring instead of fighting it every day.

You have probably told yourself, *I just need to get my act together,* more times than you can count. Maybe someone else said it, a teacher, a boss, a parent. Regardless, the message landed the same each time: *You are the problem.*

But here is the truth: You are not failing because you are less than or undisciplined. You have been trying to run someone else's race in shoes that do not fit. Blisters do not mean you are a bad runner. They mean you need different shoes.

I have seen the same story again and again. The problem is not your effort. The problem is the fit. And fit can be changed.

A NOTE ON TWICE EXCEPTIONALITY

For some, "not broken, just wired differently" has an extra layer. This is sometimes described as twice exceptionality (or 2e): having exceptional abilities and creativity alongside ADHD, learning differences, or other challenges.

This combination can be confusing. Sometimes, strengths hide the places where support is needed. Other times, struggles overshadow the gifts. From the outside, the message is often the same: *You're not living up to your potential.*

If this is you, it doesn't mean you're failing. It means your brain holds both brilliance and friction. Recognizing both sides of that truth is powerful. You're not broken; you're human and dynamic. The goal isn't to erase your challenges or ignore your gifts. It's to create a life that makes space for both.

Let's start by getting to the truth about what is really going on so you can reclaim the confidence you have been missing.

HOW WE LEARNED TO THINK WE ARE THE PROBLEM

For many of us, the earliest messages we received about how we function were anything but supportive:

- "If you just tried harder..."
- "You are so smart, but you just aren't applying yourself."
- "You have so much potential. Why are you wasting it?"

When you grow up hearing these things, you don't just question your habits. You start questioning your character.

To cope, you might:

- Mask parts of yourself that do not fit expectations
- Overcompensate until you burn out
- Live with a constant fear of messing up

In my work, I hear these stories repeatedly. Smart, capable people are constantly being told they are not living up to their potential when, in reality, they are being asked to meet expectations designed for a different kind of brain, without the right tools.

WHAT IS ACTUALLY HAPPENING

Executive functioning is not about intelligence or capability. It is a set of brain-based skills that help you:

- Plan and prioritize
- Start tasks and sustain attention
- Shift between activities
- Keep track of information and recall it when needed

- Regulate emotions and impulses

That last one, emotional regulation, is especially important to name. Many adults blame themselves for "overreacting," "being too sensitive," or "losing control," when in reality they're experiencing a normal executive function challenge. Emotional regulation is not about suppressing feelings; it's about being able to pause, notice, and respond instead of getting swept away. When this skill is supported, everything else, from planning to follow-through, becomes easier.

Executive functions fluctuate. They are stronger when you feel safe and have slept and eaten, and they are weaker when you are stressed or overwhelmed. Struggling with time management doesn't mean you lack discipline. Forgetting deadlines doesn't mean you don't care. These are skills, and like any skill, they can be supported, strengthened, or worked around.

Often, the best supports meet you exactly where the friction happens. If you forget to take your medication, put it next to the coffee maker. If you trip over shoes at the front door, put a basket there to catch them. The solution doesn't have to be perfect. It just has to work when you need it.

ACCEPTANCE AS THE FIRST TOOL

Acceptance does not mean giving up. It is telling the truth about your starting point so you can work *with* it, not *against* it.

Helpful self-talk sounds like:

- "This is how my brain works. I can support it instead of shaming it."
- "I am allowed to make things easier for myself."

Support might look like:

- Visual reminders in your line of sight
- Smaller, more realistic task lists
- Adjusting expectations to match today's capacity
- Asking for and accepting help
- Protecting systems that work for you—even if they are not considered "normal"

Acceptance also means setting boundaries. You get to say, "This works for me, so I am keeping it," even if it doesn't make sense to anyone else.

THE POWER OF UNDERSTANDING YOUR WIRING

When you stop blaming yourself, you free up mental space to build support systems.

You start to notice patterns and develop solutions. For example:

- I lose track of time in deep focus → Set timers
- I avoid tasks when I am unsure where to start → Break tasks into micro-steps
- I get more done when someone is nearby → Try working at a coffee shop or library

Your wiring is not only about challenges. It is also where your strengths live: creativity, problem-solving, spotting connections others miss, and adapting quickly in a crisis.

When you place supports exactly where something tends to break down, you spend less time fighting your brain and more time using its best features.

THINKING ABOUT YOUR FUTURE SELF

Every small choice you make today to support your brain is a gift to your future self.

Future You is the one who walks into a kitchen that's already ready to cook in. Future You can find the scissors because they are always in the same drawer. Future You is not scrambling because the bill is already paid.

It doesn't have to be big or perfect. Even a 2-minute action now can erase a 20-minute problem later.

WHY THIS MATTERS FOR NEURODIVERGENT BRAINS

When you understand that executive functioning challenges are about fit, not flaw, you can stop wasting energy on self-blame. This frees up mental and emotional resources to identify supports that work with your brain's strengths, making follow-through more likely and daily life less overwhelming.

KEY TAKEAWAYS

Core Idea: Productivity challenges are often a mismatch between your brain's needs and the strategies you are trying to use.

Big Shift: Instead of trying harder with what isn't working, experiment with tools and approaches that match how your brain actually operates.

Practical Application: Notice patterns in your energy, focus, and environment. When something feels easier, ask why and how you can recreate those conditions.

PUT IT INTO PRACTICE

Self-Talk: *My brain works differently, and I can set up systems that work for me.*

One Small Action for Future You: Set a 2-minute timer and tackle something Future You will thank you for.

Reflection: If your brain could work with you instead of against you, what would feel different in your day-to-day life?

State, Story, Strategy

A foundational tool for understanding what is going on

You sit down to work, full of good intentions. You have your coffee, your notebook, maybe even a fresh pen, because surely that will help.

But before you know it, you are 20 minutes into Instagram, or deep in your desk junk drawer, or staring at a blinking cursor.

Then, the self-talk starts: *What is wrong with me? Why am I so easily distracted? Everyone else seems to just... work.*

Here's the thing: Nothing is wrong with you. You just haven't looked at why it is hard in this moment.

When I worked in cognitive rehabilitation, I saw first-hand how brains operate differently depending on rest, stress, and environment. Later, as an ADHD and executive functioning coach, I realized most of us skip a critical step. We jump straight to doing without asking, "What is my brain working with right now?"

That is where one of my favorite frameworks comes in: State, Story, Strategy.

State is how you feel in the moment—your mood, energy level, nervous system response, and the impact of your sensory environment.

Story is the internal narrative you tell yourself, the one that can either move you into action or keep you stuck in procrastination.

Strategy is what you do—the actions, tools, or supports you use.

If your strategy doesn't fit your state, you can have the best intentions in the world and still spin your wheels. Noticing where you are first gives you a real chance to choose something that works.

State: Checking in Without Judgment

Think of state as the operating conditions for your brain. Just like you would not expect your phone to run well with 2 percent battery and 10 apps open, you cannot expect your brain to thrive without the right conditions.

Some states that make executive functioning harder include:

- **Overstimulated:** too much noise, movement, or mental input
- **Under-stimulated:** bored, sluggish, struggling to engage

- **Low energy:** tired or emotionally drained
- **Physically uncomfortable:** too hot, too cold, hungry, itchy sweater, etc.
- **Time-blind:** losing track of how long you have been on something

These are not flaws. They are conditions, and conditions can be adjusted.

Supportive self-talk: *I've noticed that I am scattered. What would help me feel grounded enough to start?*

That is not indulgence. It is setting yourself up to succeed by reducing the friction before you begin.

STORY: HOW YOU COACH YOURSELF

State is how you feel, and story is what you say to yourself.

Self-talk is your brain's internal narration, a kind of mental GPS that can either steer you toward action or send you in circles. It shapes your attention, focus, emotional regulation, and decision making. The language you use with yourself often determines whether you move forward, stall out, or spiral.

The challenge, however, is that many of us run old scripts without realizing it.

Unhelpful self-talk might sound like:

- "I'll never get this right."

- "I'm terrible at focusing."
- "I can't start until I feel ready."

These aren't just casual thoughts. They directly affect how you plan, focus, and solve problems. Often, they're inherited narratives from teachers, bosses, or family members.

The good news is that stories are editable. By shifting your self-talk, you shift the way your brain approaches tasks. You can replace old scripts with language that supports your executive functioning, such as:

- "I can start small and figure it out as I go."
- "I've done this before; I can do it again."
- "I can adjust my environment so it's easier to focus."

Intentional self-talk works because it gives your brain clear, actionable directions. Research shows that verbalizing instructions, even silently, engages the parts of the brain responsible for attention, memory, and emotional regulation. It's not fluff. It's cognitive scaffolding.

Try using self-talk to support specific executive functioning skills like:

- **Planning and Organization:** "First, I'll open the document. Then, I'll list the 3 things I need to cover."
- **Focus and Execution:** "Back to the task, one step at a time."

- **Perseverance:** "This is hard, but I can do it for 5 more minutes."
- **Flexibility and Problem-Solving:** "If this approach doesn't work, I'll try another."

When your story shifts from criticism to guidance, it changes how you show up. You're no longer just reacting to your state; you're directing it. That's the bridge between how you feel and what you do.

STRATEGY: MATCHING THE TOOL TO THE STATE

Once you know your state and story, you can pick a strategy that fits.

Some matches might look like:

- Tired but still need to work → Short burst timer, body doubling
- Overwhelmed by a big project → Break it into the first 5 minutes of action
- Distracted by noise → Noise-cancelling headphones or a quieter space
- Stuck in perfection mode → Messy first draft with no edits allowed

Not every strategy will work every time. That is not failure. That is part of the process.

Supportive self-talk: *This is my best match right now. I can adjust if it is not working.*

Bringing It Together

Here is what this looks like in real life:

- **State:** Overstimulated and anxious
- **Story:** *I cannot think straight, so I am useless today.*
- **Strategy:** Five-minute walk outside, noise-cancelling headphones, start with the easiest task

Notice that nothing here is about pushing harder. It is about matching your support to where the friction is in the moment so you can move forward with less resistance.

Why This Matters for Neurodivergent Brains

This framework is effective because it builds in a pause before action, helping you identify and address the real barrier rather than pushing through it. For neurodivergent brains, this reduces wasted effort and increases the chances of choosing strategies that lead to follow-through.

Closing Grounding Truth

Your state is not a score. Your story is not permanent. Your strategy does not have to be perfect.

This is not about fixing yourself but about giving your brain the conditions it needs to show up. When you do that, you get more done and treat yourself with the respect you have deserved all along.

 **KEY TAKEAWAYS**

Core Idea: State is how you feel. Story is what you say. Strategy is what you do. The right match between them makes your efforts more effective.

Big Shift: Instead of pushing through, start by noticing your state and adjusting your story before choosing a strategy.

Practical Application: Ask yourself: What is my state? What is the story I am telling about it? Which strategy fits both?

PUT IT INTO PRACTICE

Self-Talk: *I can choose a strategy that fits how I feel right now.*

One Small Action for Future You: Pause before starting your next task, and make one small adjustment like moving to a quieter spot, grabbing water, or rewriting your next step so it feels easier.

Reflection: How would your day feel different if you started with a state check before planning your to-do list?

Identity Shift

Why changing how you see yourself is more powerful than changing your to-do list

---

You Do Not Change by Forcing More To-Do Lists

When productivity feels impossible, the first instinct is often to change the system. You try a new planner, a new app, a new routine. Sometimes, it helps, but more often, it fades. That is because sustainable change does not start with tools. It starts with identity.

If you see yourself as someone who is always behind, no planner will stick. If you see yourself as disorganized or unreliable, it is hard to trust your own strategies. But when you shift how you think about yourself, your actions begin to line up with that new story.

Identity shift is not about pretending. It is about recognizing that the story you have been carrying may not be the whole truth. When you rewrite the story, you give yourself a new starting point.

What Is an Identity Shift?

An identity shift means moving from "I do tasks" to "I am the kind of person who..." It is the difference between saying, "I try to exercise," and saying, "I am someone who takes care of my body." Or between saying, "I want to write," and saying, "I am a writer."

Identity shapes behavior. People tend to act in ways that are consistent with how they see themselves. When you shift your identity, you create a more stable foundation than willpower alone.

WHY IDENTITY SHIFT MATTERS

Shifting identity creates alignment with your values and goals. When your sense of self matches what you are working toward, it feels less like forcing and more like living in congruence. It also creates motivation that lasts. Tools and habits come and go, but identity is sticky. You will keep returning to behaviors that confirm who you believe you are.

It also breaks shame loops. If your identity is "I am lazy" or "I am bad at follow-through," then every setback will feel like proof. But when your identity becomes "I am someone who experiments until I find what works," a broken system is not failure but simply part of the process. And because willpower alone is exhausting, identity shift helps you keep going without relying on constant force.

IDENTITY VS. LABELS YOU HAVE CARRIED

For many of us, identity has not been something we chose. It has been shaped by labels handed to us over the years: "You are so smart but lazy." "You are just not applying yourself." "If you really cared, you would try harder."

At first, these sound like critiques of behavior. But over time, they become absorbed into identity. You stop hearing, "You did not turn in your homework," and start hearing, "You are unreliable." You stop hearing, "You had trouble focusing," and start hearing, "You are undisciplined."

These labels ignore the role of executive functioning. They also ignore the impact of environments, structures, and supports.

An identity shift does not erase your past; it reframes it. "I am lazy" becomes "I am someone who works best with visual cues." "I am unreliable" becomes "I am someone who thrives with external reminders." "I am scattered" becomes "I am someone whose creativity shows up in nonlinear ways."

When you release labels that never fit, you free yourself to create identities that reflect both your challenges and your strengths.

MOVING BEYOND THE WILLPOWER TRAP

Relying on willpower alone is like trying to run a marathon without water breaks. You might last for a while, but it is not sustainable. Identity gives you a framework to lean on when motivation dips.

For example, instead of saying, "I need more willpower to start this task," try saying, "I am someone who makes things easier for myself." This small shift reframes your choices. You are no longer proving worth through effort—you are reinforcing a healthier identity with each action.

EVERY ACTION IS A VOTE

One of the most powerful parts of identity shift is realizing it is not built by one grand gesture but by one small action at a time. Writing one sentence is a vote for being a writer. Washing one plate is a vote for being someone who takes care of their space. Showing up to one meeting on time is a vote for being someone who follows through.

The votes do not need to be unanimous. You can miss a day, skip a task, or drop a ball and still maintain your identity. What matters is the direction of the evidence you are collecting. This is where "better than zero" effort matters most. Even the tiniest action is proof of identity. Over time, those small votes add up to a solid sense of self.

PRACTICAL STEPS TOWARD IDENTITY SHIFT

Start by noticing the old stories.

Pay attention to the phrases you use about yourself, like "I am always late" or "I cannot finish things." These are not just descriptions; they shape your identity.

Then, choose a new narrative that feels both true and aspirational, such as "I am someone who takes small steps forward" or "I am someone who values progress over perfection."

Finally, back it up with action. If your identity is "I am someone who finishes things," closing one browser tab counts. If your identity is "I am someone who keeps promises to myself," setting a timer and starting matters. Protect this new identity with your environment by setting reminders, creating visual cues, and designing spaces that make it easier to live out. And if you can, enlist community. Tell a friend or colleague, "I am working on seeing myself as someone who..." Sharing it can create accountability and encouragement.

THINKING ABOUT YOUR FUTURE SELF

Identity shift is not about becoming someone different. It is about aligning with the version of yourself you already want to be. Future You does not need perfection. Future You needs present you to take one action that says, "This is who I am becoming."

When you see yourself as someone who supports your brain instead of fights against it, you begin to act in ways that make that identity real. Each small step leaves evidence for Future You to look back on and say, "That is who I am."

WHY THIS MATTERS FOR NEURODIVERGENT BRAINS

When executive functioning challenges are framed as flaws, identity gets stuck in shame. By shifting identity, you reclaim your narrative. Instead of "I am failing at this," you can say, "I am someone learning to work with my brain."

This reframing matters because executive functioning

skills are inconsistent. They fluctuate with stress, sleep, environment, and support. If your identity is "I am broken when I cannot," you spiral into shame. If your identity is "I am someone who experiments and adapts," you find resilience in the inconsistency.

 KEY TAKEAWAYS

Core Idea: Identity shapes behavior more powerfully than willpower or tools alone.

Big Shift: Stop seeing yourself as broken. Start naming yourself as someone who takes small steps that align with your values.

Practical Application: Write one identity statement you aim to live by, and take a single action today that confirms it.

PUT IT INTO PRACTICE

Self-Talk: *I am someone who experiments with ways to support my brain.*

One Small Action for Future You: Choose one phrase you want to believe about yourself and practice saying it out loud.

Reflection: If you saw yourself as capable and resourceful, what would change about how you approach your day?

Productivity and Self-Worth

Untangling what you do from who you are

WHEN YOUR WORTH GETS MEASURED BY YOUR OUTPUT

For many of us, worth has been tangled up with productivity for as long as we can remember. Good grades meant you were "smart." Finishing your work before the deadline meant you were "responsible." Keeping a clean house meant you were "on top of things."

And when you missed those marks? The labels were quick to follow: *Lazy. Irresponsible. Messy.*

It is no wonder that as adults, when life feels hard to manage, we do not just question our systems, we question ourselves. Instead of "this planner doesn't work for me," it becomes "I am unreliable." Instead of "this routine is too rigid," it becomes "I am weak."

The truth is that productivity is not proof of worth. It is simply a measure of output. And output will always rise and fall depending on energy, resources, support, and season of life. Your worth is not on trial.

How the Productivity Trap Works

The productivity trap whispers, "I will feel better about myself when I finally get caught up." It insists, "I will deserve rest once everything is finished." It nags, "If I could just be consistent, I would be a better person."

But those thoughts are not motivating. They are exhausting. They create a constantly moving finish line. Even if you check every box today, tomorrow resets the list.

And the trap works because culture reinforces it. Workplaces reward overwork. Families praise "the responsible one." Productivity gets treated as a moral category. But it is not. Productivity is just output.

Why It Feels Especially Heavy
with Executive Functioning Differences

Executive functioning differences magnify this trap. When planning, task initiation, time management, or follow-through are already challenging, you will inevitably hit snags that look like failures.

Forget the appointment? "Irresponsible."

Take twice as long to finish the report? "Disorganized."

Struggle to cook dinner after a long day? "Not capable."

But none of these moments actually say anything about your worth. They are simply signals that your brain needs a different kind of support. Without that perspective, it is easy to internalize every hiccup as evidence that you are less valuable.

SHIFTING THE NARRATIVE

Untangling productivity from worth is not about lowering standards. It is about noticing the story you are telling yourself and rewriting it with compassion.

- "I cannot stay consistent, so I must not care enough." → "Consistency is harder for my brain, so I need flexible systems."
- "I cannot keep up like other people." → "My pace is different, but my contributions still matter."
- "I am only as good as what I accomplish." → "I have value no matter how much I get done."

Worth is a given. Productivity is a variable.

IDENTITY VS. OUTPUT

One of the most powerful shifts is moving from "I am what I produce" to "I am someone who shows up in ways that reflect my values."

A caring parent is not defined by whether the dishes are washed. A creative person does not stop being creative on the days they do not make art. A capable professional is not erased because they needed an extension.

When identity is rooted in values instead of output, you create space to rest, recover, and still feel like yourself.

Breaking the Cycle of Shame

The productivity–worth link often fuels a shame cycle: you struggle to keep up, judge yourself harshly, feel less motivated, fall further behind, and then use falling behind as more "proof" of low worth.

The cycle is not broken by pushing harder. It is broken by refusing to let productivity be the measuring stick for your value.

Practical Ways to Untangle Productivity and Worth

Anchor your worth in values. Write down 3 that matter to you: parent, learner, encourager, advocate. Then ask: How can I express one of these today, even in a small way, regardless of productivity?

Celebrate effort, not just output. If you sat down to write and managed 2 sentences, that is still effort worth naming. If you opened the bill, even if you did not yet pay it, that is still movement.

Plan for off-days. Instead of assuming productivity will always be steady, build in supports for when it will not be. Easy meals, buffer time, and forgiving deadlines create margin and help reinforce that your worth does not depend on flawless output.

The Role of Rest

Rest often feels like the enemy in the productivity–worth equation. If you have tied worth to output, rest feels like failure. But rest is actually a value-aligned act.

Rest makes space for creativity. Rest preserves energy for relationships. Rest prevents burnout so you can keep showing up over time.

When you see yourself as someone who values rest, it stops being indulgence and becomes part of your identity.

THINKING ABOUT YOUR FUTURE SELF

Future You does not need endless checkmarks. Future You needs a foundation of self-worth that holds steady through busy seasons and slow ones.

Picture this: One version of you ties worth to productivity. When life throws curveballs—illness, caregiving, fatigue—you spiral into shame. Another version of you ties worth to values. When life gets messy, you still know you are capable, creative, and valuable.

Which version will take better care of you? Which version is more sustainable?

WHY THIS MATTERS FOR NEURODIVERGENT BRAINS

Executive functioning differences often mean inconsistent output. If worth is tied to productivity, inconsistency feels like personal failure. Which is exactly why this shift is so important.

When worth is rooted in values, identity, and humanity rather than task completion, you free yourself from the constant cycle of shame. That reframing makes it easier to experiment with tools, try new strategies, and recover from setbacks—because your self-worth is no longer hanging in the balance.

 ## KEY TAKEAWAYS

Core Idea: Productivity is not a measure of worth. It is simply output, and output naturally fluctuates.

Big Shift: Root your identity in values instead of in how much you accomplish.

Practical Application: Replace "I was good or bad today" with neutral language. Write down 3 values that matter to you beyond productivity and look for small ways to express them.

 ## PUT IT INTO PRACTICE

Self-Talk: *My worth is steady. Productivity rises and falls.*

One Small Action for Future You: Choose one value that matters to you and complete a 5-minute action that aligns with it.

Reflection: How would your days feel different if you stopped using productivity as a scoreboard for your worth?

The Iceberg of Executive Functioning Challenges

What you see vs. what you don't

_____

THE PART EVERYONE NOTICES

When people think about executive functioning struggles, they often picture the parts that are easy to see: being late, forgetting deadlines, missing appointments, or living with constant piles of clutter. These are "above the waterline" struggles—ones visible to bosses, teachers, partners, and even strangers sometimes.

On the surface, it might look like carelessness or lack of effort. But what others do not see is the mountain of invisible effort happening beneath. Like an iceberg, the visible part is only a fraction of the whole. Beneath the surface lie layers of hidden work, frustration, and emotional toll that most people never recognize.

Understanding the full iceberg helps explain why life can feel so exhausting and why compassion and the right supports matter more than pushing harder.

BENEATH THE SURFACE: WHAT YOU DON'T SEE

Beneath those visible struggles are the parts few people notice:

- **Emotional regulation.** Small setbacks can unleash frustration, shame, or guilt. Self-regulation takes extra effort, which leaves less energy for everything else.
- **The mental load.** Invisible responsibilities, tracking schedules, remembering supplies, and anticipating needs quietly drain enormous energy.
- **The avoidance–urgency cycle.** Tasks build up from avoidance until urgency forces action. From the outside, it looks like laziness followed by a burst of energy. Inside, it feels like drowning and then gasping for air.
- **Energy fluctuations.** Some days, you move through a list with ease; other days, even starting feels impossible. That inconsistency makes reliability feel out of reach, even though it is a pattern, not a flaw.
- **The EF tax.** Late fees, duplicate purchases, and extra hours spent fixing mistakes all add hidden financial and emotional costs. Each misstep chips away at self-trust.
- **Sleep and rest struggles.** Racing thoughts and trouble winding down keep you from the very rest your brain needs to function well. The cycle compounds exhaustion.
- **Self-worth wounds.** Years of being told to "try harder" leave scars. Beneath the surface sits

the belief that something must be wrong with you, even when the reality is far more complex.

WHY THE ICEBERG METAPHOR MATTERS

The iceberg explains why executive functioning challenges are so often misunderstood. People see the tip—missed deadlines, messy spaces—and assume it is the whole story. But most of the weight—the shame, the invisible labor, the constant re-regulation—is hidden beneath.

When you see the whole iceberg, judgment can be replaced with compassion. Supports can be placed where they matter most: beneath the surface, not just at the tip.

REFRAMING THE EF TAX

The hidden costs of executive functioning challenges can feel discouraging, but naming them is the first step toward reducing them. The EF tax shows up in late fees and replacement costs, in hours lost to redoing tasks, and in the guilt of yet another apology.

You are not alone in paying this tax. And while it may never disappear entirely, small systems can chip away at it: Automated bill pay. A basket by the door for keys. Visual reminders that catch your eye. Gentle accountability from someone you trust.

Each safeguard lightens the hidden weight.

Practical Strategies to Navigate the Iceberg

You do not have to face the whole iceberg at once. Start with supports that target the hidden layers such as:

- Externalizing memory with alarms, whiteboards, or visual cues
- Simplifying choices to reduce decision fatigue
- Breaking tasks into small, specific steps that feel doable
- Automating where you can with recurring payments or orders
- Building in recovery time instead of expecting constant output
- Practicing compassionate self-talk (*This is a skills challenge, not a character flaw*)

Each of these supports chips away at what lies beneath the waterline, leaving more energy for what matters most.

THINKING ABOUT YOUR FUTURE SELF

Future You does not need perfection. Future You needs systems that keep the iceberg from pulling you under. A reminder on your phone. A basket for the mail. A routine you can manage even on tired days. Every support helps.

WHY THIS MATTERS FOR NEURODIVERGENT BRAINS

When executive functioning challenges are misunderstood, people carry not just the iceberg itself but also the shame of being judged for it. Naming the hidden parts removes some of that weight. It helps you see yourself not as lazy or incapable but as someone whose brain needs different tools. That shift builds compassion for yourself and for others navigating similar struggles. And compassion is what makes lasting change possible.

 # KEY TAKEAWAYS

Core Idea: Executive functioning challenges are like an iceberg. Most of the weight lies beneath the surface, unseen.

Big Shift: Instead of focusing only on the visible struggles, recognize the hidden layers and place supports where they matter most.

Practical Application: Identify one executive function tax you're paying this week and take one quick action to reduce it.

 # PUT IT INTO PRACTICE

Self-Talk: *My struggles are not the whole story. There is more happening beneath the surface.*

One Small Action for Future You: Choose a hidden cost like late fees, lost items, or wasted time and create a recurring support or habit today so it's easier to avoid in the future.

Reflection: If others could see the full iceberg of your experience, how would you want them to respond differently?

Invisible and Emotional Labor

The unseen work that drains executive functioning

_____

WHEN YOU ARE EXHAUSTED BUT CANNOT NAME WHY

There are days you collapse into bed, body heavy, mind foggy, and if someone asked what you accomplished, you would struggle to answer. You might glance at the dishes still in the sink or the email inbox left uncleared and wonder, *What did I even do today?*

Here is the truth: You did a lot. But much of it was invisible.

Invisible and emotional labor is the background work that keeps life stitched together. It does not produce neat checkmarks on a list or applause from anyone else, but it quietly demands your focus, energy, and self-regulation. And when executive functioning is already working overtime, this hidden work can be the very thing that leaves you drained before the day is half over.

What Invisible Labor Looks Like

Invisible labor is the mental spinning that keeps everything else running. It is not just folding laundry. It is noticing the kids have outgrown their socks, remembering to add them to the grocery list, and realizing the drawer will not close until you declutter last season's clothes.

It is not just showing up at the birthday party. It is RSVPing on time, buying the present, finding the wrapping paper, and making sure everyone is dressed and in the car.

Invisible labor rarely gets recognized because it is the pre-work of life—the planning, tracking, and anticipating that allows visible work to happen at all.

What Emotional Labor Looks Like

Emotional labor is the parallel work of tending to feelings, both yours and everyone else's. It is biting your tongue in a meeting so things do not escalate. It is softening your tone with a partner who is already stressed. It is listening to your child's worries while silently carrying your own.

Sometimes, emotional labor is chosen as an act of care, a way to strengthen relationships. Other times, it piles up quietly until you realize you are monitoring the emotional climate of every room you enter, smoothing rough edges, and absorbing tension like a sponge. That effort rarely shows, but it costs energy all the same.

WHY INVISIBLE AND EMOTIONAL LABOR HIT SO HARD

Executive functioning skills such as planning, prioritizing, shifting, and emotional regulation are the gears that keep life moving. Invisible and emotional labor tug at all of them at once.

Working memory gets clogged when you are carrying everyone's schedules in your head. Prioritization crumbles when every need feels urgent because it belongs to someone else. Task initiation stumbles when the work has no clear start or finish. Emotional regulation stretches thin when you are absorbing other people's stress and pushing down your own.

And because this work is unseen, it rarely earns acknowledgment. That lack of recognition makes the load feel even heavier. You are not only carrying the labor itself, but you are also carrying it alone.

THE EMOTIONAL TOLL

The exhaustion from invisible and emotional labor is not just physical; it is emotional. You might feel resentment toward others who seem oblivious to the weight you are holding. You might feel guilt for not "doing enough," even when you are already at capacity. You might compare yourself to people who appear to handle it better and conclude you are just bad at life.

This self-blame deepens the fatigue. It tells you the problem is not the load; it is you. But the truth is, the work you are doing is real. It is simply invisible to the outside world.

WHY NAMING IT MATTERS

When you name invisible and emotional labor, you make it visible. Visibility is the first step toward compassion, both for yourself and from others. Naming it helps you stop blaming yourself for being tired when the load was real all along. It gives you the language to ask for help or renegotiate responsibilities instead of silently shouldering them. It allows you to set boundaries about what is truly yours to carry. And it helps you place supports where the actual friction is, instead of scolding yourself for not trying harder.

While naming does not make the work disappear, it does make it manageable. It turns a fog into something you can map, plan for, and share.

A STORY YOU MIGHT RECOGNIZE

Think of a parent who keeps track of school forms, doctor's appointments, grocery lists, after-school activities, and family birthdays. On paper, the day looks like they "just went to work and made dinner." But in reality, they have been coordinating, adjusting, and solving problems since dawn.

Or picture a professional who leaves a meeting feeling inexplicably depleted. They did not just contribute their expertise. They also spent the entire hour gauging tone, softening conflict, and keeping the conversation on track. That invisible role of "emotional anchor" was labor too, even if it did not show up in the meeting minutes.

Invisible and emotional labor weave through daily life so seamlessly that even you might not notice you are doing it, until you start to name it.

What You Can Do About It

You cannot eliminate all invisible or emotional labor, but you can make it more visible, shared, and sustainable.

Start by getting it out of your head. Write down the mental load you are carrying this week, everything from "remember to RSVP" to "check if the dog's meds are running low." Seeing it in front of you makes it easier to decide what to keep, what to share, and what to drop.

Then, practice using validating language. Instead of brushing it off with "It is not a big deal, I will just handle it," try saying, "I am coordinating a lot right now" or "I have been doing a lot of background work this week." That language helps others see the load and helps you honor it.

Next, notice your patterns. Do you default to smoothing emotions? Do you automatically hold everyone's schedules? Patterns are not destiny. Once you see them, you can decide whether they serve you or whether they need a boundary.

Finally, schedule recovery. Because this work never truly ends, you have to end it yourself. That might mean a walk after a tense conversation, silence between meetings, or setting aside non-negotiable downtime. Rest is part of the system.

GENTLE SELF-REFLECTION: WHAT IS YOURS TO CARRY?

Invisible and emotional labor can feel endless, but not all of it belongs to you. Ask yourself: Which pieces could someone else take on if I stopped carrying them by default? Which expectations have I inherited but never agreed to? Where could I lower the bar and still honor my values?

These are not easy questions, but they create space. And space is what executive functioning thrives on.

THINKING ABOUT YOUR FUTURE SELF

Future You does not need you to do it all. Future You needs systems that carry some of the weight automatically. That might look like a shared digital calendar, a recurring grocery delivery, or a clear launch pad where everyone's things live.

It also means protecting Future You's energy by setting boundaries now. Saying "I cannot be the one who tracks this anymore" may feel uncomfortable, but it is an act of care—for both the present and future version of yourself.

WHY THIS MATTERS FOR NEURODIVERGENT BRAINS

For people with executive functioning differences, invisible and emotional labor does not just add weight; it multiplies the friction. Every unacknowledged task pulls at working memory, every unspoken responsibility drains regulation, and every hidden demand chips away at focus.

When the work remains invisible, so does your effort. Naming it brings dignity back to the labor you have been doing all along. It reframes exhaustion not as failure but as the natural outcome of carrying more than meets the eye.

 ## KEY TAKEAWAYS

Core Idea: Invisible and emotional labor are real, heavy, and uncredited. They drain executive functioning.

Big Shift: Stop treating exhaustion as weakness. Recognize the unseen load and make it visible.

Practical Application: Write down the invisible labor you're carrying this week. Pick one task to share, delegate, or set a boundary around today.

 ## PUT IT INTO PRACTICE

Self-Talk: *The work I carry counts, even when no one sees it.*

One Small Action for Future You: Do a 5-minute brain dump of all hidden tasks on your mind. Identify one recurring type of task and create a strategy to simplify, share, or let it go long-term.

Reflection: If others could see the invisible labor you are carrying, what would you want them to understand?

Energy Management

Why fuel, rest, and rhythms matter more than willpower

WHEN TIME MANAGEMENT ISN'T ENOUGH

If you've ever sat down with a perfectly planned day and still couldn't follow through, you already know the truth: time management isn't the whole story.

Time is neutral. Energy is what makes time usable.

You can have an open hour on your calendar, but if you're depleted, foggy, or restless, that hour won't translate into progress. On the flip side, even a short burst of focused energy can sometimes do more than a whole free afternoon.

That's why energy management matters more than willpower. It's the missing layer underneath calendars and to-do lists. When you understand your rhythms and fuel your body and mind, you stop asking your brain to perform on empty.

WHAT ENERGY MANAGEMENT REALLY MEANS

Energy management is noticing and supporting the

natural ebbs and flows of your focus, stamina, and motivation. It isn't about being "high energy" all the time but about aligning tasks with the energy you *do* have and making choices that protect it.

For people with executive functioning challenges, this shift is powerful. Time management often assumes steady output, which is an unrealistic expectation when your brain runs in bursts, dips, or cycles. Energy management meets you where you are.

THE FOUR ANCHORS OF ENERGY

Energy isn't random. It's influenced by 4 key anchors:

1. **Sleep**. Sleep is the foundation of cognitive function. Without it, working memory falters, attention wavers, and emotional regulation frays. Many adults struggle with "tired but wired" evenings or inconsistent routines that make sleep difficult. That's not laziness; it's wiring. Prioritizing calming wind-down rituals and consistent wake times can be more impactful than any productivity hack.

2. **Fuel**. Nutrition directly affects focus and mood. Long gaps without eating, skipped meals, or heavy sugar spikes send energy on a roller coaster. Simple, steady fuel, balanced meals, snacks that combine protein and carbs, and hydration keeps energy stable. You don't need perfection; you need predictability.

3. **Movement**. Physical activity isn't just about fitness; it's also an energy regulator. Movement

burns off restlessness, boosts dopamine, and clears mental fog. This doesn't have to mean long workouts. It can mean stretching, a walk around the block, or dancing in the kitchen. Short bursts sprinkled throughout the day reset focus more effectively than hours of white-knuckled concentration.

4. **Rest and recovery**. Rest isn't wasted time. It's how your nervous system resets. Without recovery, your brain runs hot, and executive functions crash. Rest can look like naps, meditation, hobbies, or simply sitting quietly without input. Even micro-rest, like closing your eyes for 2 minutes or breathing deeply, can make a difference.

JOY AND CONNECTION: THE OVERLOOKED FUEL

Energy doesn't just come from managing the basics; it also comes from what fills you up. Joy, play, and meaningful connection are renewable energy sources that often get overlooked in the name of productivity.

Think about the difference between dragging yourself through chores and spending 10 minutes laughing on the phone with a friend. One drains you, while the other restores you. Joy doesn't require hours, it can be a song you love, a shared joke, a quick walk with a neighbor, or a hobby that absorbs you in flow.

For brains that often feel weighed down by obligations, fun isn't frivolous. It's fuel. Building in moments of joy and connection isn't just good for your spirit; it literally supports focus, resilience, and stamina.

Daily Rhythms: Noticing Your Peaks and Valleys

Everyone has natural rhythms. Maybe mornings are clear-headed, afternoons slump, evenings spark creativity. The trouble comes when you schedule tasks against your rhythm instead of with it.

Energy management means noticing patterns and aligning work accordingly. For example:

- Use peak energy for creative or strategic tasks.
- Place routine or admin tasks in lower-energy slots.
- Build in recovery after energy-heavy events like meetings or caregiving.

This isn't indulgence; it's efficiency. It's how you protect your best energy for what matters.

Working With Bigger Rhythms

Energy isn't just daily. It's weekly, seasonal, and even life-stage.

Some people peak early in the week and need lighter Fridays. Others find energy builds slowly, making mid-week their sweet spot.

Seasons shift capacity too: long summer days feel expansive, while winter invites slower rhythms.

Life seasons matter as well. Parenting young kids,

caregiving for aging parents, or navigating perimen-opause can all change the baseline.

When you zoom out, you see that low energy isn't fail-ure; it's a rhythm. Planning with bigger cycles in mind helps you expect dips instead of being surprised by them.

WHY WILLPOWER ISN'T THE ANSWER

Most of us have tried powering through low-energy moments with willpower. The result? Tasks take longer, mistakes multiply, and shame spirals begin. Willpower is a fragile fuel. It's drained by decisions, stress, and fatigue. Energy management is renewable, meaning it builds a cycle of replenishing instead of depleting.

PLANS ARE TENTATIVE—SHIFT THEM WITH INTENTION

Traditional productivity advice treats plans as con-tracts: if you write it down, you must follow it exactly. But when energy is your real resource, rigidity backfires.

Plans are not promises. They are intentions. Shifting them when your energy changes is not a failure; it's wise. The key is to shift with intention, not avoidance.

For instance, skipping a workout because you're exhausted may feel like failure. But intentionally swapping it for a walk and earlier bedtime is energy management. Likewise, postponing deep work because your brain is fried may feel lazy. But intention-ally moving it to tomorrow morning, when you know you'll be sharper, is a strategy.

The goal is not to stick to every plan but to steward energy wisely so you can keep moving forward over time.

A Story You Might Recognize

Imagine this: You block 3 hours to finish a big project. You sit down after lunch, determined. Ten minutes in, your eyelids are heavy, your focus drifts, and everything feels harder than it should. You blame yourself: *Why can't I just push through?*

Now, picture a different approach. You notice afternoons are your low point, so you start the day with the project while your mind is sharper. You plan a short walk after lunch to reset. By the time the slump arrives, you're doing lighter tasks like email and prep for tomorrow. You end the day with energy left, not completely drained.

Same number of hours. Completely different results.

Practical Ways to Support Your Energy

- **Protect sleep.** This is non-negotiable. Even 15 minutes of extra rest changes your day.
- **Fuel steadily.** Don't wait until you're running on fumes; steady snacks keep energy smooth.
- **Move often.** Short bursts of activity reset focus better than hours of force.
- **Use transition rituals.** Tea, a short walk, or tidying a desk signals your brain to reset.
- **Schedule recovery.** Plan downtime as intentionally as work. It's not optional; it's fuel.

- **Make space for joy.** Add one small moment of connection or play into your day—a song, a text, a laugh, a hobby. Fun restores energy as much as sleep and food.

THINKING ABOUT YOUR FUTURE SELF

Future You doesn't need you to squeeze more into every hour. Future You needs a brain and body that aren't running on fumes. When you manage energy, you create sustainable capacity. Tasks get done with less friction, and setbacks don't feel like collapse.

Picture Future You walking into a day with steady reserves: sleep banked, meals planned, recovery scheduled, joy sprinkled in. That version of you doesn't need to rely on willpower. They're supported.

WHY THIS MATTERS FOR NEURODIVERGENT BRAINS

When executive functioning is inconsistent, energy dips hit harder. A rough night of sleep or a skipped meal can unravel focus and follow-through. That's why managing energy isn't optional; it's foundational. By framing energy—not time—as the real resource, you give yourself permission to care for your body, rhythms, and joy as part of productivity, not separate from it.

 KEY TAKEAWAYS

Core Idea: Energy—not time—is the real currency of productivity.

Big Shift: Stop forcing willpower; align tasks with your natural rhythms and allow plans to shift with intention.

Practical Application: Track your daily, weekly, and seasonal energy patterns for one week. Adjust your plan around what you notice.

🎯 PUT IT INTO PRACTICE

Self-Talk: *Plans are flexible. Protecting my energy is a strategy, not a failure.*

One Small Action for Future You: Add one small moment of fun or connection to today, a song, a laugh, or a check-in with a friend.

Reflection: If you treated energy, not time, as your most valuable resource, how would you plan your day, your week, or your season differently?

You Do Not Need to Do It Like Everyone Else

Letting go of one right way

You try someone's "perfect morning routine" you heard about on a podcast.

Day one feels fresh.

Day 2, you are dragging, but you push through.

Day 3, you skip it and immediately think: *What is wrong with me? It works for everyone else.*

Here is the reframe: The problem is not you. The problem is that you are trying to live inside someone else's structure.

Your brain was not built to fit every system, and that's okay. You don't have to copy someone else's approach to be successful. In fact, the best systems are the ones you create for yourself, ones that work *with* your brain instead of *against* it.

THE PRESSURE TO CONFORM

From school to workplace culture to social media, the world sends constant messages about the "right" way to plan, clean, parent, or work.

That pressure feels even heavier when your brain works differently. Executive functioning—mental skills that help you plan, prioritize, remember, initiate, regulate, and follow through—does not always pair well with rigid schedules, traditional task lists, or "start with the hardest thing" advice.

When you have been told there is only one right way to do things, every failed attempt at a standard method can feel like proof you are lazy, disorganized, or not trying hard enough. Over time, that can lead to:

- Repeating strategies that never stick
- Blaming yourself for inconsistency
- Avoiding tasks altogether because it feels pointless

Opting out of systems that drain you is not giving up. It is choosing a path where your effort actually has a chance to succeed.

WHEN BEST PRACTICES DO NOT WORK FOR YOU

Most popular productivity tips assume:

- Neurotypical energy patterns
- Unlimited willpower
- Linear, predictable workflows

If that is not your reality, those so-called best practices can feel exhausting and demoralizing.

Supportive self-talk: *It is okay that I need different tools to get to the same outcome.*

FLEXIBILITY IN TIME, PLACE, AND MANNER
You do not have to do things in the same time, place, or manner as anyone else.

Time
Let go of the idea that there is a "right" time.

- Meal prep at 9pm if that is when you have energy.
- Plan your week on Thursday if your brain needs a ramp-up period.

Place
Tasks do not have to stay in their official spaces.

- Write from a coffee shop if the background buzz helps you focus.
- Sort laundry while watching TV if movement and noise keep you engaged.

Manner
Work in bursts instead of long stretches.

- Use sticky notes instead of a planner.
- Break a big task into scattered 10-minute chunks rather than forcing one long block.

These are not shortcuts. They are personalized systems that meet you where the friction happens.

BUILDING YOUR OWN PLAYBOOK

Borrow ideas from others, but treat them like test drives. Keep what works, discard what does not, and leave guilt out of it.

When collaborating, communicate your needs clearly: "I cannot keep up with that tracking system, but here is another way I can give you the information you need."

Real-life examples:

- A night owl who plans their week at 11pm because that is when they think most clearly
- Someone who keeps 2 calendars, one traditional and one made entirely of sticky notes, because it finally gives them the visual overview they need
- Laundry that only gets folded if it is done at night in front of the TV instead of in the laundry room during the day

Your systems will evolve over time, not because you failed, but because your needs and seasons change. That is normal.

PROTECTING YOUR UNIQUE SYSTEMS

Once you find what works, resist pressure to "upgrade" to someone else's shiny new method.

Supportive self-talk: *Different is not less. It is tailored.*

It is okay to politely decline when someone tries to "fix" a system that already works for you.

WHY THIS MATTERS FOR NEURODIVERGENT BRAINS

When you give yourself permission to design systems around your brain instead of trying to fit into rigid norms, you reduce wasted energy and increase follow-through. For neurodivergent brains, this flexibility can mean the difference between abandoning a task and completing it with less stress.

CLOSING GROUNDING TRUTH

There is no gold star for doing things the "normal" way and no penalty for doing them your way. If the conventional methods have not worked for you, maybe it is not you. Maybe it is time to trust that your way is valid because it is.

 # KEY TAKEAWAYS

Core Idea: You do not have to match someone else's time, place, or method to be successful.

Big Shift: Redefine "best practices" as "best for me practices."

Practical Application: Adjust one task this

week in its timing, location, or method. Notice how your follow-through changes.

🎯 PUT IT INTO PRACTICE

Self-Talk: *If it works for me, it works.*

One Small Action for Future You: Create a go-to plan for one recurring task. Set it at the time, place, or manner that usually works best for your brain so it happens more easily and with less friction in the future.

Reflection: What am I ready to stop doing just because everyone else does it that way?

Decision Making That Fits Your Brain

Finding clarity without the pressure of perfect

───────────────────────────────

WHY DECISIONS FEEL HARD

Everyday life is filled with decisions. Some are small: what to make for dinner, when to send that email, whether to do laundry today or tomorrow. Others feel weighty: which career move to pursue, how to manage money, what school to choose for your child. For people with executive functioning differences, both the small and the large choices can feel exhausting.

Decision making pulls on several executive functioning skills at once: planning, prioritizing, working memory, and emotional regulation. When those skills are already under strain, even simple choices can feel like holding a remote with too many buttons. You just want to turn on the TV, but the sheer number of options makes you freeze. That's why you might find yourself staring at a takeout menu for 20 minutes, too drained to pick, or putting off an important decision until urgency finally forces your hand.

THE INVISIBLE LOAD OF CHOICES

We often underestimate the sheer number of choices we make in a day. Should I answer this text now or later? Should I take the long route or the short one? Do I say yes to the invitation or make an excuse? Each tiny choice might not seem like much on its own, but together, they create decision fatigue—a slow depletion of your mental energy.

Decision fatigue is real, and it especially impacts people with executive functioning differences. When your working memory is full, prioritization skills stretched, and emotional regulation taxed, your brain does not just get tired; it gets stuck. Stuck in avoidance. Stuck in "what ifs." Stuck in the loop of second-guessing.

This is why decisions can feel heavier than they look. It is not only about choosing between A and B. It is about the mental effort required to sort, evaluate, anticipate, and regulate your emotions about the choice. That invisible load matters.

WHY "PERFECT" TRIPS US UP

One of the biggest obstacles in decision making is the belief that you must make the perfect choice. Perfectionism magnifies every decision into a high-stakes test. If you choose wrong, you will waste time, lose opportunities, or prove you are not capable. That pressure locks you in place.

The truth, however, is that very few decisions are permanent. Most are experiments. Even the big ones often allow for course correction. Waiting for certainty before acting often costs more than making a good-enough choice and adjusting along the way.

When you are chasing perfection, you may put off deciding until urgency forces action. By then, the decision is made in panic rather than with intention.

BRAIN-FRIENDLY WAYS TO DECIDE

Decision making does not have to drain you. With the right supports, you can make choices that feel lighter, faster, and more aligned with your values.

Shrink the Decision

Big, vague decisions create overwhelm. Shrink them until they feel concrete.

- Instead of "get healthier," decide "I will schedule one doctor's appointment this month."
- Instead of "be more productive," decide "I will write down 3 priorities before opening my email."
- Instead of "organize the garage," decide "I will clear one shelf this weekend."

Small choices add up. They also give your brain the dopamine hit of progress which fuels momentum.

Use External Supports

You do not have to keep the whole decision in your head. Get it out into the open by:

- Making a quick pros and cons list
- Asking a trusted friend to talk through the options
- Writing each option on a sticky note and move them around until one feels lighter

Externalizing reduces the load on working memory and helps you see the decision with fresh eyes.

Try Micro-Decisions

Big decisions can be broken into a series of small, low-pressure ones.

- "Should I change careers?" → "Should I research one new field this week?"
- "Should we move?" → "Should I look at houses online in 2 neighborhoods?"

Micro-decisions create forward motion without locking you in.

Lean into Defaults and Routines

Not every choice deserves your full energy. If you eat the same breakfast every day, that is not boring; it is strategic. Default routines conserve decision-making power for the choices that matter most.

GENTLE EXPERIMENTS, NOT FOREVER CHOICES

One of the kindest ways to approach decision making is by reframing choices as experiments. You are not signing a lifelong contract. You are trying something to see what you learn.

When you treat a decision as an experiment, you free yourself from the pressure of forever. You can say, "I will try this system for 2 weeks," or "I will test this strategy for a month and then reassess." This mindset reduces fear of failure and increases flexibility.

Experiments build data. Each trial gives you information about what works, what doesn't, and what you want to adjust. The outcome is not success or failure but learning.

THINKING ABOUT YOUR FUTURE SELF

Future You does not need you to make flawless choices today. Future You benefits from choices that create movement, even if small. When you choose to try something, you give Future You information, momentum, and often relief.

Future You is less stuck because present you chose to move forward. Future You trusts you more because you showed up, even if imperfectly. That is the real finish line in decision making: building trust with yourself.

WHY THIS MATTERS FOR NEURODIVERGENT BRAINS

For people with executive functioning differences, decision making can be one of the stickiest places. The combination of time blindness, emotional intensity, working memory overload, and perfectionism can keep you spinning.

Using strategies like shrinking the decision, externalizing it, or treating it as an experiment lowers the friction. It makes the decision fit your brain instead of demanding your brain fit the decision. That shift is powerful. It transforms decision making from a source of dread into a skill you can trust yourself with.

 ## KEY TAKEAWAYS

Core Idea: Decision making is not about finding perfect answers. It is about creating forward motion in ways that fit your brain.

Big Shift: Choices are rarely permanent. Most are experiments, and each one teaches you something.

Practical Application: When you feel stuck, shrink the decision to the smallest possible next step.

 ## PUT IT INTO PRACTICE

Self-Talk: *I do not need the perfect choice. I need the next choice.*

One Small Action for Future You: Pick one decision you have been avoiding. Redefine it as a micro-decision and take that step today.

Reflection: If I treated this decision as an experiment, how would that change the way I approach it?

PART TWO

THE MYTH OF CONSISTENCY

Why productivity advice doesn't work for everyone and what to do instead

Accumulation Over Consistency

Making progress without consistency

You clean the bathroom once, then not again for 3 weeks, and you think, *I can never stick to anything.*

Here is the reframe: The bathroom is still cleaner than if you had never touched it. The effort counts, even when it is inconsistent.

Let us shift from an all-or-nothing view of progress to one that recognizes how small, occasional actions, especially intentional ones, build up over time.

THE PROBLEM WITH CONSISTENCY MYTHS

Productivity culture often tells us consistency is the gold standard. Daily habits, perfect streaks, and never missing a day are held up as the ultimate signs of success.

For many brains, life moves in waves of high energy followed by periods of rest or distraction. When you miss a day, the shame cycle begins. You start strong, skip a few, and then quit altogether because you believe you have ruined it.

For many neurodivergent adults, freedom, choice, and authenticity are not luxuries. They are required for meaningful work. Rigid rules and repetitive routines can feel like cages, even when you desire the outcome they promise. Forcing yourself into someone else's mold often backfires. Creating systems that honor your autonomy matters more than keeping a streak alive.

Example: You try a 30-day workout challenge and complete the first week, but a sick child or urgent work project interrupts your schedule. The old mindset says, *I ruined it.* The accumulation mindset says, *Those 7 workouts still count, and I can add more later.*

WHAT ACCUMULATION LOOKS LIKE

Accumulation means that small, spaced-out actions still add up over time.

It might look like:

- Reading 3 books a year because you only read in summer
- Organizing a drawer every few months
- Doing stretches a few times a week instead of every day

Example: You meal prep once a month when you have the energy. That still gives you 12 weeks a year when you avoid midweek dinner chaos.

Protect your right to choose what "enough" looks like for you, even if others believe it is too little.

Why Accumulation Works

Every action helps you avoid sliding all the way back to the beginning, even if it happens weeks apart. That's because accumulated actions build a foundation over time, and each round of effort makes the next one lighter and faster.

Accumulation works best when it is intentional. You might clean the kitchen because you want a calmer morning tomorrow, or organize your desk to focus better on your next project. When bursts connect to your values or goals, you create more lasting motivation, making it easier to return after breaks.

Supportive self-talk: *I may not do this every day, but every time I do it, I move forward.*

Example: You deep-clean the fridge every few months. Each time it takes less work because there is less buildup, and your future self benefits from every round.

Celebrating Bursts

Track effort in ways that measure total actions rather than streaks.

- Give yourself credit for any action toward the goal—no matter how small.
- Notice and celebrate when something takes less effort than it did last time.

- Avoid letting apps, planners, or other people measure your success only by frequency. You decide what progress looks like.

Example: Instead of crossing off a daily box, keep a tally of total walks you have taken this month. Even if they are spread out, seeing the number grow shows you it is adding up.

PLANNING FOR YOUR NATURAL RHYTHM

Notice when you are most likely to have more energy—whether it is morning bursts, weekend afternoons, or a random Tuesday night—and lean into it.

Instead of forcing yourself to work daily, plan to ride the waves when they come.

Have replacement strategies ready for when your current method stops working. If your daily checklist no longer grabs your attention, swap it for sticky notes, a whiteboard, or voice memos. The goal is not to force yourself back into what failed but to keep moving forward with tools that work for you now.

Build in light restart rituals to reduce the friction of starting again. A tidy desk, a fresh notebook page, or a quick calendar review can help you re-enter without resistance.

Example: You do not journal every day, but when the urge strikes, you grab your favorite pen, light a candle, and make a cup of tea. That mini-ritual makes it easier to restart without guilt.

Why This Matters for Neurodivergent Brains

Shifting from a perfection-based model to an accumulation mindset helps reduce shame and makes it easier to restart after breaks. For neurodivergent brains, this flexibility increases the likelihood of sustained progress and prevents the all-or-nothing crashes that come from unrealistic consistency standards.

Closing Grounding Truth

You do not need to do something every day for it to matter. Your progress might zigzag, stall, or leap forward in unexpected ways. That is normal. It is still forward motion.

Every action you take counts toward the life you are building. Accumulation is still progress.

 KEY TAKEAWAYS

Core Idea: Small, spaced-out actions build up over time.

Big Shift: Replace perfect consistency with intentional accumulation.

Practical Application: Choose one goal and add to it in bursts this week. No streak required.

⊙ PUT IT INTO PRACTICE

Self-Talk: *If I do it, it counts.*

One Small Action for Future You: Set something up today so you can start easier next time.

Reflection: Where am I holding myself to an impossible daily standard that I could replace with an "every so often is enough" mindset?

Slow Progress Is Still Progress

Letting go of the fast or fail mindset

You finally start cleaning out the closet that has been on your mind for months.

You take everything out, feeling energized by the sight of a clean, empty space. You make piles, sorting through sweaters you forgot you owned and shoes you have not worn in years.

Halfway through, your brain says no. Decision fatigue creeps in, and your focus scatters, but the floor is still covered in clothes. So you leave it for the day.

It sits like that for a while, maybe a few days, maybe longer. Life piles on, the mess spreads, and the closet area looks even more chaotic than when you began. But when you do come back, it's easier to reset to where you left off and add a little more progress. Each round feels a bit lighter.

Finally, after a few sessions spread out over time, you

close the closet door on a job well done. And your first thought is, *That took way too long. I am so scattered.*

Here is the reframe: Slower progress is not less valuable. In fact, it is often more sustainable, especially when your brain does not operate in a straight line. This is not about speed, neatness, or meeting an invisible deadline. It is about moving forward, even if it happens in smaller, slower, or less predictable steps.

THE MYTH OF FAST PROGRESS

We live in a culture that celebrates speed. Faster deadlines. Quicker turnarounds. Instant results. Success is often measured by how quickly something is completed.

For anyone with ADHD or executive functioning differences, progress often comes in bursts, cycles, or winding paths that do not match the "start to finish in one sitting" model. Some days, your brain might sprint, and other days, it might crawl.

When you judge your pace against someone else's, you create a direct path to burnout and shame. And shame is one of the quickest ways to shut down motivation altogether.

WHAT SLOW PROGRESS LOOKS LIKE IN REAL LIFE

Slow progress can be hard to recognize because it does not always look impressive in the moment. It might look like:

- Chipping away at a project 10 minutes at a time
- Taking breaks between stages of a task because your brain or body needs recovery time
- Spending months building a habit, and mostly keeping it once it sticks
- Needing more steps than others to get to the same outcome
- Returning to a task multiple times before it is complete

This stop-and-start pattern is not a weakness. It is often your brain's natural way of managing energy, decision making, and attention over time.

If you feel frustration creeping in, try the State, Story, Strategy lens from an earlier chapter:

- **State:** What is your energy, mood, or sensory load like right now?
- **Story:** Are you telling yourself you are too slow? If so, could you reframe it as pacing yourself for sustainability?
- **Strategy:** What is one small action that matches your state today and reduces friction?

THE BENEFITS OF GOING SLOW

When you move at a pace your brain can sustain, you:

- Reduce the risk of overwhelm, which makes finishing more likely

- Give yourself space for creativity, problem-solving, and finding better approaches along the way
- Manage your energy so you are not recovering from a sprint for days afterward
- Build habits and systems that last instead of collapsing after a burst of intense effort

Supportive self-talk: *Moving at a pace I can sustain is smarter than rushing to burnout.*

How to Recognize and Celebrate Incremental Wins

If you only celebrate when something is completely finished, you miss hundreds of opportunities to boost motivation along the way.

Try:

- Tracking your progress visually with lists, check-ins, or before-and-after photos
- Giving yourself partial credit for moving something forward, even if it is not finished yet
- Treating restarts as proof you are still in the game, not evidence of failure
- Acknowledging that small, repeated actions compound into real change over time

When others are involved, communicate your process and pace up front so they know what to expect.

Letting Go of Comparison

When you see someone else finish faster, it is easy to think you are behind. But you are comparing your reality to their highlight reel.

They have their own pace, resources, and wiring. You have yours.

Supportive self-talk: *They have their pace. I have mine. My pace works for me.*

WHY THIS MATTERS FOR NEURODIVERGENT BRAINS

Honoring your natural pace allows you to work with your brain's energy cycles instead of against them. For neurodivergent brains, this reduces burnout, builds confidence, and makes it more likely that you will stick with a project long enough to finish it.

CLOSING GROUNDING TRUTH

Speed does not determine value. If you took even one step closer to where you want to be today, no matter how small, then you made progress.

 # KEY TAKEAWAYS

Core Idea: Progress is progress, no matter the pace. Small, steady, or inconsistent steps all still count.

Big Shift: Redefine success by the direction you are moving, not the speed you are taking.

Practical Application: Notice when you are moving forward, no matter how small the step, and keep a simple log of these moments. Review it regularly to remind yourself that progress is building, even if it feels slow in the day-to-day.

 PUT IT INTO PRACTICE

Self-Talk: *Slow progress is sustainable progress.*

One Small Action for Future You: Write down one thing you moved forward today, no matter how tiny.

Reflection: How would your work feel different if you valued every step toward your goals instead of only the finish line?

You Do Not Have to Do It the Same Way Every Time

Adjusting your methods to maintain momentum

———————————————————

Last week, you prepped healthy lunches on Sunday. This week, you grabbed takeout twice and assembled sandwiches on the fly.

The common thought is, *I cannot stick to anything.*

Here is the reframe: Flexibility is not proof that you have failed. It is a skill that keeps you moving when life shifts. Changes in approach are often adaptive problem-solving, not backsliding.

THE CONSISTENCY TRAP

Productivity culture often tells us to pick one method and stick with it forever.

For ADHD and other executive functioning differences, this advice can be a trap. Life circumstances change. Energy and focus levels rise and fall. Your physical environment might be different from one week to the next.

When your brain and life are naturally variable, locking yourself into one fixed method can create unnecessary stress. Instead of helping you stay on track, it can make you feel boxed in, resentful, or ready to abandon the task entirely.

Giving yourself permission to adapt is not a sign of weakness. It is recognition that your mind works best when it can respond to changing needs.

Example: You start using a digital budget tracker in January but check it less often by March. Switching to a paper notebook keeps you more consistent because you see it daily on your desk. The format changes, but the goal is still being met.

WHY FLEXIBILITY WORKS

Flexibility keeps progress alive when the original plan no longer matches your reality. It allows you to work with your current state rather than against it. Adjusting your methods reduces friction and makes it easier to take the next step.

Flexibility also opens the door to experimentation. You can try new tools, environments, or time frames. Notice which ones support you best in different situations and act accordingly.

Supportive self-talk: *I am adjusting because I am paying attention and shifting.*

Example: You plan to work from your home office but

feel restless and distracted. Instead of forcing your-self to push through, you move to a library or coffee shop and finish the work there. You complete the task because you adapted.

REAL-LIFE EXAMPLES OF FLEXIBLE APPROACHES

Flexibility is easier when you have a ready list of options you can rotate between. Think of it as a menu of strategies for different areas of life.

Work Tasks
- Keep a paper notebook for weeks when you crave the satisfaction of writing things down.
- Use a digital task list when you need reminders or quick reordering.
- Record a voice memo when typing feels like too much.

Meal Prep
- Cook big batches on weekends when you have time and energy.
- Prep only snacks or breakfast items during busier weeks.
- Choose takeout or simple frozen meals when cooking is not feasible.

Household Chores
- Focus on one room at a time on low-energy days.
- Use a 15-minute timer to make progress in short bursts.
- Hire help or trade chores with someone else

when you feel overwhelmed.

Exercise
- Take a 20-minute walk when the weather is nice.
- Do a dance video or home workout when you want to stay inside.
- Choose gentle movement like stretching or yoga on low-energy days.

The more options you have ready, the less time you spend feeling stuck.

AVOIDING THE ALL-OR-NOTHING SPIRAL
Flexibility is helpful, but it can slip into avoidance.

Signs you might be avoiding rather than adapting include:

- Constantly switching approaches without taking meaningful action
- Spending more time researching the perfect method than actually starting

When you notice this happening, use a mini reset. Instead of trying to restart perfectly, pick the smallest next step that moves you forward.

Supportive self-talk: *This week's version is good enough to keep me moving.*

Example: If you skipped your planned workout and

cannot do the full session, walk around the block or stretch for 5 minutes. Small adjustments keep you connected to your goal without the pressure of perfection.

Building a Flexibility Mindset

Expect variation instead of resisting it. There's rarely just one way to finish a task, especially since what works best often depends on the situation.

Create a menu of approaches for recurring tasks. Include methods you have used successfully before, even if they are not your current habit. The next time one option stops working, you can quickly switch to another instead of starting from scratch.

When you are working with others, communicate changes simply and directly. For example: "I am changing how I am doing this so I can keep it moving." This protects your right to adapt while reassuring others you are still committed to the outcome.

Example: For staying in touch with friends, your menu might include voice notes during your commute, quick text check-ins during busy weeks, or monthly coffee dates when you have more time. All are valid ways to maintain connection.

Why This Matters for Neurodivergent Brains

Flexibility allows you to work with changing energy levels, attention spans, and environments without losing momentum. For neurodivergent brains, having multiple ways to approach a task prevents burnout,

keeps engagement higher, and makes it easier to follow through even when circumstances shift.

Closing Grounding Truth

Doing something differently does not mean you are
doing it wrong. It means you are willing to adapt so you
can keep going, and that is what success looks like.

 # KEY TAKEAWAYS

Core Idea: Flexibility is a proactive strategy
that keeps you in motion.

Big Shift: Changing your method is a form of
problem-solving, not a sign of failure.

Practical Application: Choose one task you
want to do often and create a list of 3 different ways you could approach it.

 # PUT IT INTO PRACTICE

Self-Talk: *I am allowed to change the
method if it keeps me moving.*

One Small Action for Future You: Add a new
option to your menu for a habit or routine
you care about.

Reflection: Where am I forcing myself to do something one way when another way might work better right now?

Letting Go of Productivity Guilt

Making peace with rest, slowness, and unmet expectations

You finally sit down to rest, but your brain has other plans.

A mental scroll starts playing: the laundry you have not folded, the emails you still need to answer, the tasks you promised yourself you would finish. Instead of relaxing, you feel your shoulders tighten. You tell yourself, *I should be doing something.*

This nagging sense that you are not doing enough is productivity guilt.

The irony is that this guilt does not make you more productive. It drains energy, fuels burnout, and chips away at self-trust. To break free from it, you have to untangle your sense of worth from your output and learn to see rest and joy as legitimate, valuable parts of the process.

What Productivity Guilt Really Is

Productivity guilt is the feeling that you are falling short, the constant hum of "not enough" in the background of your mind.

Culturally, we are taught to measure value in terms of busyness and output. Busy people are praised. Resting people are questioned. For adults with ADHD or executive functioning challenges, inconsistent productivity can be misread by others and by yourself as laziness or lack of effort. That misunderstanding fuels a cycle of overcompensating when you have energy and shaming yourself when you do not.

Productivity guilt often carries an unspoken message: *If I am not producing, I am not valuable.* But the truth is quite the opposite. You are valuable because you exist—not because you check enough boxes.

Example: You spend an afternoon helping a friend move but still feel guilty at night because your work inbox is full. You dismiss the meaningful effort you gave because it did not "count" in the way productivity culture defines it.

How Guilt Backfires

Guilt turns rest into restless waiting. You sit down to recharge, but your mind keeps calculating what you "should" be doing instead. You never get the benefits of the break because you cannot stop thinking about the work.

It also pushes you into the burnout cycle. You over-compensate when you feel guilty, push past your natural limits, and then crash harder. Over time, this roller coaster erodes motivation. Instead of building trust in your ability to follow through, you reinforce the belief that you can only function when you are making up for lost time.

This same guilt can also steal joy from hobbies and fun activities. Instead of losing yourself in a game with your kids, painting, or enjoying a walk with a friend, you catch yourself thinking, *I should be doing something more productive.* Over time, this mindset trains your brain to view joy as optional instead of essential.

THE ROLE OF ACCEPTANCE AND SUPPORT

Letting go of productivity guilt starts with internal acceptance: *I am allowed to rest, and I am allowed to have fun without "earning" it.*

Rest is not a prize you give yourself after enough output. It is the fuel that makes future output possible. Fun is not a distraction. It is nourishment for creativity, relationships, and well-being.

It also helps to have external support—people who understand your rhythms and do not measure your value by your busyness. This might be a friend who reminds you that taking a day off is normal or a coworker who respects your boundaries without questioning them.

To challenge guilt-driven thoughts and make space for a different narrative, use self-talk phrases such as:

- Rest is part of getting things done.
- Fun is part of a sustainable life.
- I am not behind; I am pacing myself, and things are never finished.
- This pause is an investment, not a waste.

PRACTICAL WAYS TO LET GO OF GUILT

- Schedule rest and fun like any other task and keep the appointment.
- Keep a "done list" to counteract the feeling of "I have done nothing."
- Give credit for every step forward, even small ones.
- Replace "should" with "could" in your self-talk.

Example: If you normally clean the whole kitchen at once but today you only load the dishwasher, you still acknowledge that as progress. If you normally spend Saturday mornings running errands but choose to go to the park with a friend, you recognize that joy has value too.

BOUNDARIES PROTECT YOUR ENERGY AND JOY

Your energy is finite, and protecting it is an act of self-respect. Here are a few ways to set some boundaries:

- Say no without over-explaining.
- Communicate your capacity honestly: *I do not have the bandwidth for that right now.*

- Build in recovery and joy time after high-output days or weeks.

Example: If you finish a big work project on Friday, keep Saturday light and do something fun that has nothing to do with your to-do list. Resist the temptation to fill that time with catch-up tasks.

Why This Matters for Neurodivergent Brains

For all brains—but especially neurodivergent ones—rest and joy are not rewards but essential components of functioning well. Guilt creates mental noise that drains energy needed for focus and follow-through. Letting go of productivity guilt preserves motivation, builds resilience, and makes your work cycles more sustainable.

Closing Grounding Truth

You do not need to earn rest, and you do not need to justify fun. You are a whole, functional person, whether or not you cross off every item on today's list. Productivity is not proof of your worth, and guilt has no role in your value.

 **KEY TAKEAWAYS**

Core Idea: Your worth is not tied to your pro-ductivity. Guilt drains energy and joy without improving output.

Big Shift: Rest and fun are essential parts of a sustainable life.

Practical Application: Build both rest and joy into your week and protect them as fiercely as any other commitment.

🎯 PUT IT INTO PRACTICE

Self-Talk: *My value is not measured by my output.*

One Small Action for Future You: Schedule one block of time this week for something fun that has no practical purpose.

Reflection: If you woke up tomorrow feeling completely at peace with how much you were doing, with no guilt about rest or fun, what would you notice first?

The Lies We Tell Ourselves

Turning false promises into cues for action

"I will wake up early tomorrow and get it done."

Morning comes, and the bed wins.

We all make little promises to our future selves—ones we genuinely believe in the moment—only to watch them dissolve when it is time to act. These moments are not proof of laziness or lack of willpower. They are your brain's way of hoping you will feel different later. That is human.

The good news is you can use these moments as cues, not to judge yourself but to adjust your plan to something actually doable for the brain you have today.

WHY WE MAKE THESE PROMISES

When you picture Future You, you often imagine someone with more energy, motivation, organization, and discipline than the version of you who exists right now. That imagined self feels unstoppable, so you assign them unrealistic tasks.

For people with executive functioning challenges, it is common to:

- Underestimate how long things take
- Overestimate how much energy you will have
- Avoid discomfort now in favor of something easier in the moment

When comfort is only a tap away in the form of snacks, scrolling, or "just one more episode," your brain gets a quick hit of dopamine. It feels good now but does not move you closer to your goal.

Spotting Your Favorite Lies

These little promises can take many forms, such as:

- I will start tomorrow.
- I just need to feel more ready.
- I work better under pressure.
- I need everything to be perfect before I begin.
- I do not have time right now.
- I will do it after one more episode or scroll.
- I will wake up early tomorrow morning.
- I will never be able to do this.

It is tempting to label these as purely self-sabotage, but that is not the full story. They are coping mechanisms—ways your brain tries to avoid overwhelm or discomfort. You do not need to judge yourself for them. You only need to notice them with curiosity.

FROM LIE TO CUE: MAKING A DIFFERENT PLAN

Every time you catch yourself making one of these promises, pause. This is your cue to make a plan for the real you in this moment, not for the mythical Future You with unlimited energy.

Replace:

- "I will wake up early" with "I will set a timer for 10 minutes right now and just start"
- "I need everything to be perfect" with "I will do a quick, imperfect version now and refine it later"
- "I do not have time" with "I can do 5 minutes today, which is still progress"

This is how you find the middle ground. You do not give up entirely, but you also do not set a standard so high it becomes unreachable.

MAKE IT SMALLER AND MORE VISIBLE

When you shrink the first step, you lower the amount of energy your brain needs to get going. Pair that with supports that make it easier to start like:

- Working alongside someone for built-in accountability
- Keeping what you need to do in sight so it stays on your radar
- Using reminders and alarms
- Matching harder tasks with times when your energy is naturally higher

THE POWER OF ACCOUNTABILITY AND SUPPORT

Sometimes, you cannot get unstuck on your own. This is where accountability partners and support systems make the difference.

An accountability partner can:

- Give you an objective perspective on what is realistic
- Check in to help you stay on track
- Offer encouragement when you feel stalled

Choose someone you trust, who will be consistent and supportive without judgment. Even a short "I am about to start" message can make it easier to follow through.

Support can also come from:

- A friend or coworker who knows your patterns
- Online groups where you work alongside others
- A coach or therapist who helps you plan for your actual capacity

EFFECTIVE GENTLE SELF-TALK

Notice how much easier follow-through becomes when your inner voice is on your side. Try saying:

- "Mornings are not my best time, so I will plan for the afternoons."
- "I do not need to be perfect to make progress."
- "Five minutes counts."

- "I can do something now and make it better later."

Self-awareness is a form of support. The more you understand your patterns, the less you will expect your brain to be something it is not, and the more you will set yourself up to succeed.

WHY THIS MATTERS FOR NEURODIVERGENT BRAINS

For neurodivergent brains, unrealistic promises to Future You can create shame when they are not kept. Treating them as cues instead of failures shifts the focus from perfection to progress. This approach reduces avoidance, builds trust in your follow-through, and helps you plan for your actual energy and capacity.

CLOSING GROUNDING TRUTH

The lies we tell ourselves are not proof that we are lazy. They are proof we still have hope that things can be different. And that hope is worth protecting.

When you treat these lies as cues to make smaller, doable plans, you turn them into stepping stones instead of stumbling blocks.

Start now. Not with the whole thing. Not with a perfect plan. Start with one small action Future You will thank you for.

 **KEY TAKEAWAYS**

Core Idea: Every "lie" is a cue to redesign the plan so you can take a real step now.

Big Shift: Your patterns are not proof you cannot change. They are clues for building a better plan.

Practical Application: The moment you notice a future promise, create a smaller, doable action that fits your current energy and environment.

 **PUT IT INTO PRACTICE**

Self-Talk: *I can use this as a signal, not a judgment.*

One Small Action for Future You: Next time you catch yourself thinking "I'll do it later," finish one small step before you stand up, and decide exactly when "later" will be.

Reflection: When in the past have you turned a "later" into a "now," and what helped you do it?

Rupture and Repair

How to restart when systems break

It is going so well... until it is not.

One week, you are in a groove with meal prep, laundry, workouts, everything ticking along. The next week, you are eating cereal for dinner, digging socks out of the dryer, and wondering when you last opened your planner.

If you struggle with executive functioning, this shift often feels like it happened overnight, and it is tempting to see it as proof you cannot stick with anything. But systems are not machines. They are more like houseplants. They thrive with regular care, but they can survive a stretch of neglect. And when they start to droop, the answer is not shame but attention.

UNDERSTANDING RUPTURE

A rupture is when a system you rely on stops working or you stop using it.

With a houseplant, you might see dry soil, drooping

leaves, or a little layer of dust. None of that means it is dead. It means it needs care.

For those with executive functioning differences, rupture is almost inevitable. Life changes. Energy shifts. Interest cycles. A system that felt effortless last month can suddenly feel like pushing a car uphill. This is not a flaw within you. It is the natural rhythm of how your brain interacts with structure.

WHY RUPTURE HAPPENS (AND HOW TO REPAIR EACH ONE)

Life Interruptions: illness, travel, or intense work deadlines.

When life pulls you away from your routines, it is normal to return and find them collapsed.

Repair Strategy: Restart gently. Pick one small anchor task to reestablish first. If travel derailed your meal routine, start with restocking a few easy groceries. If illness set you back on housework, choose one room or surface to reset before moving on.

Executive Functioning Shifts: burnout, decision fatigue, or sensory overwhelm.

These shifts often mean your system is asking more of you than you have the energy to give right now.

Repair Strategy: Strip your system down to its easiest version. If your task list is too long, replace it with a short must-do-today list. If cooking feels impossible, rotate through 3 easy meals for a while. The goal is less decision making so you can get traction again.

Changes in Priorities or Interests: your old system feels heavy and unhelpful.

When your life shifts, your old routines can start to feel like the wrong fit.

Repair Strategy: Redesign to fit your current reality. If your elaborate planner no longer works, try a sticky note or index card. If your workout plan bores you, swap it for something you look forward to. Keep what still serves you and let the rest go.

Sometimes, it is not neglect at all. The season simply changes, and your "plant" needs something different. It might need more water in the summer and less in the winter. Systems work the same way.

THE REPAIR MINDSET

The most important part of repair is to start small. You do not need a full overhaul. One supportive step is enough to bring life back.

Think of plant care as a model for system care:

- **Water it.** Do one small action to get things moving again. Start a load of laundry. Clear just your desktop. Open your planner and write down one thing.

- **Trim the dead leaves.** Let go of the backlog that no longer matters. Archive old emails. Recycle the pile of flyers. Cross off the to-dos you know you will not do.
- **Move it to better light.** Adjust your environment or approach to match what is true right now. Maybe you fold laundry in the living room instead of the bedroom. Maybe you work at a café instead of your desk.

The goal is not perfection. It is momentum.

PLANNING FOR FUTURE RUPTURES

Since rupture is inevitable, plan for it.

- Expect that systems will need rewatering and build in checkpoints.
- Learn your early warning signs such as missed days, avoidance, or dread.
- Respond early, before the system collapses entirely.

You would not get mad at a plant for needing water. You would notice and respond. Treat yourself the same way.

GENTLE SELF-TALK DURING REPAIR

Replace "I cannot stick with anything" with "This worked for me for a while, but now it needs an adjustment."

Rupture does not erase progress. Reviving a wilted plant does not send it back to seed; it continues from where it is. Your systems are the same.

Why This Matters for Neurodivergent Brains

Ruptures are part of the natural cycle for neurodivergent brains, not a sign of failure. Viewing them as opportunities for repair rather than proof of inadequacy preserves momentum, reduces shame, and makes it easier to re-engage with systems after a break.

Closing Grounding Truth

Your systems are not meant to last forever without change. They are living things that grow, adapt, and sometimes take a nap. What matters is not that they break, but that you notice, respond, and keep going.

 **KEY TAKEAWAYS**

Core Idea: Systems are like plants. They do not fail when they wilt; they simply need care.

Big Shift: A rupture is not the end of a system. It is part of its natural cycle.

Practical Application: Restart with one small supportive action, clear what no longer matters, and make an adjustment that fits your current reality.

PUT IT INTO PRACTICE

Self-Talk: *My systems are living things. They can be revived.*

One Small Action for Future You: Pick one system that feels wilted and give it 5 minutes of care today.

Reflection: If you approached your broken systems like a plant that could be revived, what is the first small action you would take to bring it back to life?

PART THREE

TOOLS THAT ACTUALLY HELP

*Supports that meet your brain
where it is*

External Supports Are Not Cheating

How to work with your brain instead of against it

——————————————————————

I used to let clean laundry sit in the basket for days. Putting it away felt like the most boring, never-ending part of the whole process. Now I make it a game. If I have a meeting coming up, I set a short timer and challenge myself to see how much I can put away before it goes off.

Using a timer made me realize how quickly I can get this done. I often accomplish far more in a short burst than it feels like I can. That timer is an external support. It gives me structure, urgency, and a clear finish line. It gives my brain the nudge it needs to start, because once I am in motion, the rest usually follows.

Timers, sticky notes, body doubling, and alarms are not shortcuts. They are tools.

WHY SUPPORT CAN FEEL LIKE A STEP BACKWARD

If you grew up being told to "remember your homework" or "go clean your room," having an alarm or a sticky note as an adult can feel like being back in childhood. You might even hear your own inner voice saying, *Shouldn't I be able to do this without help by now?*

The truth is everyone uses supports. People keep calendars, write grocery lists, and set phone reminders. When you have executive functioning challenges, the supports you need might be more visible, frequent, or creative than the ones other people use. That does not make them childish. It makes them intentional.

When a pilot uses a pre-flight checklist, no one questions their competence. Your brain deserves the same courtesy.

Real Life Swap
Instead of: *I should remember this on my own.*

Try: Writing it down the moment you think of it.

WHAT EXTERNAL SUPPORTS ACTUALLY DO

External supports work because they:

- Reduce the need to hold information in working memory
- Interrupt distraction before it spirals
- Create cues in your environment that guide you toward action

Without these tools, you might spend more energy keeping track of the things you need to do than actually doing them.

Real Life Swap

Instead of: *I will remember to reply to that email later.*

Try: Leaving the draft open with a subject line so it is ready when you return.

Choosing the Right Support for the Moment

The best support is the one that fits the exact challenge in front of you.

- **Struggle with starting:** body doubling (working alongside someone in person or virtually to create shared focus), a countdown timer, or the "just 5 minutes" rule
- **Forget mid-task:** sticky notes, visible checklists, or on-screen prompts
- **Lose track of priorities:** a visual task board or a single sticky note with your top 3 tasks

The Sticky Note That Saved a Meeting

I was headed into a meeting and knew there was one key point I could not forget to bring up. Normally, I would trust myself to remember, and often, I would not. This time, I grabbed a sticky note and wrote the point in big letters. I set it right on my notebook.

Halfway through the meeting, my mind wandered. When my turn came, my eyes landed on the sticky note. That one small action made the difference between keeping the thought in my head and actually getting it into the conversation.

This worked because visible cues take the load off working memory. You can focus on what is happening now instead of rehearsing a reminder in your head.

Real Life Swap
Instead of: *I will just keep it in mind until the meeting.*

Try: Writing it down and placing it where you will see it at the exact moment you need it.

RELEASING THE STIGMA AROUND SUPPORT
Many of us picked up the idea that if a tool is too helpful, it means we are not "really" doing the work. That is like telling someone who wears glasses they should just "see better."

Neurodivergent brains often do not respond to willpower alone. They respond to environments, cues, and supports that make it easier to act. Using those supports is not a backup plan. It is the plan.

Real Life Swap
Instead of: *I will just try harder next time.*

Try: Adding a reminder, cue, or support that makes trying harder unnecessary.

GENTLE BOUNDARIES AND SELF-TALK
When you notice yourself resisting a tool because it feels too "extra," try reframing it. Replace:

- "I should not need this" with "This works for my

brain, so I am going to use it"
- "I will just keep track of it in my head" with "I will make it visible so my brain does not have to work so hard"
- Hiding your supports with using them openly and modeling them for others

Allow yourself to be resourced the same way you would want for someone you care about.

Why This Matters for Neurodivergent Brains
External supports reduce the cognitive load that makes task initiation, memory, and follow-through harder. For neurodivergent brains, visible cues and structured tools replace the need to rely on willpower, making success more consistent and less exhausting.

Closing Grounding Truth
Different tools, same principle: find the support that gets you moving and use it without apology.

External supports are like glasses for your brain. You would not tell someone to "see better" without glasses. Stop telling yourself to "focus harder" without the tools that make it possible.

 KEY TAKEAWAYS

Core Idea: External supports are strategic tools that work with your brain instead of against it.

Big Shift: Tools do not make you less capable; they make you more effective.

Practical Application: Match the tool to the specific challenge, whether that is starting, remembering, or staying focused.

PUT IT INTO PRACTICE

Self-Talk: *I am not less capable for using this. I am smart for knowing it helps.*

One Small Action for Future You: Choose one task today and pair it with a support, such as a timer, sticky note, or reminder alarm.

Reflection: What is one tool that has worked for you in the past, and how could you use it again this week to make something easier?

Cycle Through Strategies

How to experiment, choose your defaults, and adapt when life changes

―――――――――――――――――――――――

Every 3 months, a note pops up on my calendar: *Rework your strategies.*

It is my cue to pause and ask, *What is working for me right now, and what is not?*

My brain does not do "set it and forget it." It does "set it and check back later." I regularly cycle through how I meal plan, how I exercise, and how I start my mornings.

Sometimes, I make big changes. Other times, if something is still working well, I keep it for another season. The point is not to overhaul everything just because the date changed. It is to be proactive instead of waiting until I am frustrated or burned out.

Cycling through strategies is not about chasing the next shiny thing. It is about noticing what still serves you and letting go of what does not—*without* guilt.

WHY WE KEEP SWITCHING

For many people with executive functioning challenges, a new system or tool feels exciting. It brings novelty, which can deliver a burst of dopamine. That "fresh start" energy can make a new strategy feel like this might finally be "the one."

Strategies can stop working for a few reasons:

- Your needs have shifted.
- You did not give it enough time to become familiar.
- Your life circumstances have changed.

Changing your approach is not failure. It is a sign that you are paying attention to yourself.

Real Life Swap

Instead of: "I must have been wrong to try this in the first place"

Try: It worked for me until it did not. Now I can choose something that works better.

EXPERIMENT WITH YOUR TIMING

My seasonal reminder works for me, but that does not mean it is right for you. Some people refresh their strategies every month, while others can go a year or more before something needs adjusting.

Think of it like changing a filter. Some environments require more frequent swaps than others. If you always hit a wall in the same place, then take it as your signal to check whether the timing of your strategy refresh needs to change. Put the support where the friction shows up.

Real Life Swap
Instead of: Waiting until you are burned out to change your system.

Try: Scheduling a quick check-in every month to ask, "What feels clunky right now?"

Name Your Red Flags

How do you know when it is time to swap a strategy? Look for your personal "it is not working" signals.

Mine are:

- Avoiding a task I used to breeze through
- Feeling more dread than usual to start
- Inventing reasons to procrastinate

Your red flags might be different. The point is to catch them early so you can make a small change instead of waiting for a full crash.

Real Life Swap
Instead of: "I will just push through until this gets unbearable."

Try: "What is one support I could swap out right now to make things lighter?"

CHOOSE YOUR DEFAULTS

Defaults are your go-to moves—the things you do automatically, so you don't waste energy deciding.

Examples:
- Eating the same quick breakfast on weekdays
- Declaring Friday afternoon as your email cleanout time
- Keeping scissors in one consistent spot

Benefits of Defaults:
- Reduce decision fatigue
- Free up working memory
- Support follow-through by removing small daily choices

Real Life Swap
Instead of: "What should I eat for breakfast today?"

Try: "I have my weekday breakfast ready to go, and I save variety for the weekend."

HOW DEFAULTS FIT INTO STRATEGY CYCLING

Defaults aren't forever commitments. They're "good for now" placeholders you can lean on until they stop working. When they do, simply swap them out for something that fits better.

That seasonal reminder on my calendar keeps me from clinging to a method just because it used to work. It also helps me notice when something still feels good and keep it going without overthinking.

The gift of a good default is predictability. It gives you steady ground in one area of life so you have more energy left for the parts that are always shifting.

Real Life Swap
Instead of: "I have to commit to this forever."

Try: "This works for now, and I will change it when I need to."

Always Use Something
You do not have to stick with the same strategy all the time, but it will make life easier.

The method can change. The intentional use of support should stay.

Real Life Swap
Instead of: "I will just wing it until I find the perfect system."

Try: "I will keep using something that helps me, even if I change it later."

Gentle Boundaries With Yourself
When you choose a strategy or default, it does not have to be perfect. It only needs to be helpful for where you are now.

Helpful Self-Talk:
- "I am picking this because it works for me right now."

- "I do not need a perfect system to make progress."
- "It is fine to start small instead of overhauling everything."

Real Life Swap
Instead of: "If I cannot do it perfectly, I should not bother."

Try: "If it helps even a little, it is worth trying."

WHY THIS MATTERS FOR NEURODIVERGENT BRAINS
For ADHD and other executive functioning differences, strategies are rarely "set and forget." Energy levels, focus, and motivation shift with seasons, stress, and interest. Cycling through strategies lets you adapt before burnout hits, keeping systems supportive without the mental drain of starting from scratch every time.

CLOSING GROUNDING TRUTH
Cycling through strategies is not proof you cannot commit. It is proof you are willing to keep adapting until you find what works for the season you are in. Keep what is working until you need something new. Then, swap without guilt when life changes.

 **KEY TAKEAWAYS**

Core Idea: Strategies can and should evolve with you.

Big Shift: Changing your approach does not mean you failed; it means you are paying attention to what works.

Practical Application: Use defaults to save energy and refresh them when they no longer fit.

◎ PUT IT INTO PRACTICE

Self-Talk: *I can choose what works for now and change it when I need to.*

One Small Action for Future You: Set a recurring reminder at your chosen interval to rework your strategies.

Reflection: What are your personal red flags that let you know when a strategy is losing its edge?

Design Your Environment, Not Just Your To-Do List

How sensory input, visibility, and structure shape behavior

The only plants I reliably remember to water are the ones on my shower windowsill. Not because I love them more, but because I see them every day. The others, tucked away on a high shelf or in the corner, fade into the background until it's too late. Just kidding, my husband usually keeps them alive.

That is the thing about follow-through. It is not just about discipline or motivation. It is about making the right thing the easy thing.

When you set up your environment to work with your brain, it is like building a silent partner into your day, one that keeps nudging you forward without constant pep talks or sheer willpower.

WHY ENVIRONMENT MATTERS

Many people with executive functioning challenges know what they want to do, but they still cannot seem to get themselves to do it. This is not laziness. Your brain responds to what you can see, hear, feel, and access.

If something is invisible, hard to reach, or wrapped in extra steps, follow-through drops. If something is obvious, appealing, and easy, follow-through rises.

Think about vitamins. If they are in a closed cabinet, you might forget them entirely. If they are in a bright little dish next to your coffee maker, you are far more likely to take them every morning without a second thought.

Sensory Input

Your environment is communicating with your brain all the time. Light, sound, scent, and texture send cues that either make action easier or harder.

Bright light in the kitchen can cue your body to start meal prep. White noise can help your mind tune out distractions. Clearing visual clutter off a desk can make your brain relax enough to focus. A soft blanket can make reading time feel like something to look forward to instead of another item on a list.

One client of mine always procrastinated evening clean-up until she added warm under-cabinet lights in her kitchen. The glow made her feel cozy instead of drained, and she found herself wiping counters and loading the dishwasher almost automatically.

If there is a specific place where you consistently stall,

like a dark desk corner where you dread working, then change something in that spot instead of telling yourself to push through. Adjust the lighting, add a plant, or switch your chair. Put the support exactly where the friction happens.

Visibility

"Out of sight, out of mind" is not just a saying. For ADHD brains, it is practically a law.

Clear storage bins make art supplies easy to find. A laundry basket in the room where you actually change clothes means fewer piles on the floor. Setting out workout clothes on a chair the night before makes them far more likely to end up on your body the next day.

Visibility also works in reverse. If something is a distraction, hide it. Keep tempting snacks out of reach if they derail your focus. Move your phone out of your line of sight during work.

One of my clients struggled to remember paperwork deadlines. Now she keeps a bright, see-through folder labeled "This Week" right on her desk. It is in her way enough to keep her on track without creating visual chaos.

Structure

Structure does not mean strict rules or rigid schedules. It means making the next step easy and obvious.

Physical structure might be a launch pad by the door for your keys, wallet, and sunglasses. Time structure might be a specific day each week when you handle bills or meal prep.

When scissors have one clear home, you do not waste time hunting them down. When Friday afternoon is your "clear the inbox" time, you stop wondering when it will get done.

Structure frees up mental bandwidth. The less you have to think about when or where to start, the more energy you have to actually do the thing.

LIFE RHYTHMS

Rhythms are patterns that repeat without a lot of conscious effort. They are similar to routines but more flexible. Laundry every Sunday. A quick fridge clean-out before grocery shopping. Morning coffee paired with reviewing your day's plan.

Routines are fixed, like exercising at 7am sharp. Rhythms flex—like moving your body most afternoons, even if the exact time changes.

One way to make rhythms stick is to attach them to something you already do. If you want to add stretching into your day, pair it with brewing coffee instead of forcing it into a random slot in your schedule.

PUTTING IT ALL TOGETHER

When you combine sensory cues, visibility, structure,

and rhythms, you are making action the easiest possible next step.

Picture this: Your desk is well-lit and clear except for the project you are working on. Your calendar has a set focus block each afternoon. Your to-do list for that block is already visible.

In this setup, there is no wasted energy deciding where to start. Your environment is already pointing you toward the next move.

WHY THIS MATTERS FOR NEURODIVERGENT BRAINS

Executive functioning is heavily influenced by environmental cues. For neurodivergent brains, the right setup can act like scaffolding, reducing the mental load, making next steps visible, and minimizing the need for willpower. A supportive environment is not a luxury; it is a tool that directly impacts follow-through.

CLOSING GROUNDING TRUTH

You're not stuck because you're broken or lazy. You just haven't set things up to give your brain a little extra support. When your space carries some of the weight, the work doesn't magically disappear; it just feels lighter, more doable, and a whole lot less like pushing uphill. Setting up your environment to reduce friction and add cues gives your brain a clear path forward, so the work happens with less resistance and more ease.

KEY TAKEAWAYS

Core Idea: Your environment influences your behavior more than motivation alone ever will.

Big Shift: Instead of relying on willpower, make desired actions visible, accessible, and appealing.

Practical Application: Use sensory cues, visibility, structure, and rhythms to make follow-through easier and more automatic.

PUT IT INTO PRACTICE

Self-Talk: *I can shape my environment so it works with me, not against me.*

One Small Action for Future You: Change one thing in your space this week to make a task easier to start.

Reflection: Which space already nudges you toward action? Where could you borrow that same approach for something you have been avoiding?

Not Starting vs. Can't Keep Going

A guide to identifying needs instead of pushing through

———————————————————

The other day, I found myself staring at the same email for what felt like forever. My eyes were technically reading, but my brain was somewhere else entirely. I kept thinking, *Come on, just get through it.*

Nothing happened. Not a single sentence.

It wasn't that I didn't care or didn't know what to say. My brain simply didn't have what it needed to work. I got up, grabbed a snack, stepped outside into the sunlight for a minute, and just like that, the fog began to lift. My brain hadn't been "lazy." It had been out of fuel.

When your energy, mood, and nervous system are in a good place, your brain has what it needs to plan, prioritize, and follow through. When something essential is missing, even the simplest task can feel like climbing a hill with a backpack full of bricks.

That moment reminded me of something I've learned over and over: Usually, it's not about trying harder. It's about asking, *What's missing?* and listening for the answer.

Two Kinds of Stuck

There's not starting, where you want to get going but can't find traction. You circle the task in your head, shuffle papers, open the tab then close it again.

Then, there's can't keep going, where you've burned through your energy tank. Even the smallest step feels like a marathon.

Knowing which kind of "stuck" you're in matters because the way forward is different.

What Your Brain Needs to Work

To function well, your brain needs:

- **Energy:** enough physical stamina to think and do
- **Emotional regulation:** the ability to feel without being completely derailed
- **Nervous system balance:** not being stuck in fight, flight, or freeze
- **Cognitive flexibility:** the ability to shift when life changes

If one of these is low, your brain isn't failing you. It's sending you a signal.

THE "WHAT'S MISSING?" CHECK

Before you muscle through, pause and ask yourself:

- **Rest:** Have I slept or had any downtime?
- **Fuel:** Do I need food, water, or movement?
- **Clarity:** Do I know exactly what the next step is?
- **Support:** Would help, accountability, or company make this easier?
- **Stimulation:** Could novelty, variety, or sensory input bring me back online?

This isn't procrastination. It's preparation, making sure you have the resources to actually do the work.

RESETS IN REAL LIFE

When something feels off, it's often not about will-power. Your brain is simply missing a key ingredient. Spot the gap, meet the need, and you can shift from stuck to steady surprisingly fast.

- **Missing rest?** One client told me they "powered through" a report by sheer determination... but it took all afternoon. The next time they noticed the same brain fog, they stepped away for a 20-minute break in the sun. They finished the task in half the time.
- **Missing fuel?** I once spent an hour fussing with a spreadsheet before realizing I hadn't eaten since breakfast. Ten minutes and a snack later, I was moving again. I now keep almonds and fruit where I work so I can refuel without losing momentum.

- **Missing clarity?** "Clean garage" might live on your to-do list for months because it's too big. Shrink it to the smallest visible step like "move recycling bin outside," and you'll often keep going once you start.
- **Missing support?** A friend uses virtual body doubling whenever she's stalled. Just knowing someone else is working alongside her keeps her from slipping back into avoidance.
- **Missing stimulation?** If you've been in the same chair all day, changing your environment can flip the switch. Sometimes, I'll move to a sunny corner of the room and put on a playlist. Ten minutes later, my brain is back online.

If you consistently stall in a certain spot, like the desk in your bedroom, put your "missing" support right there. That might mean keeping snacks in the drawer, a clock in your line of sight, or a list of micro-steps taped where you can see it.

PROTECTING YOUR ENERGY

Treat your best energy like a limited resource. Use it for what matters most, not the low-priority tasks that will drain you for no reason.

Supportive self-talk: *My limits are information, not a flaw.*

THE "STOP AND SWAP" HABIT

When you start to stall:

1. Stop instead of forcing it.
2. Check what's missing.
3. Swap in the support you need.

The more often you do this, the less you'll see stuck moments as failure. They become cues—signals you know how to respond to.

Why This Matters for Neurodivergent Brains

Executive functioning relies on having enough cognitive, emotional, and physical resources to initiate and sustain tasks. For neurodivergent brains, these resources can fluctuate quickly. Recognizing what's missing before pushing through helps preserve energy and makes follow-through more realistic.

Closing Grounding Truth

Every stuck moment is a signal. Learning to pause, check in, and reset isn't a detour; it's the most direct route to sustainable progress.

 KEY TAKEAWAYS

Core Idea: Stalling out is often a sign that a resource is missing, not that you are failing.

Big Shift: Your brain is not broken; it is responding to its conditions. Meet the need and your skills can work the way they're meant to.

Practical Application: Pick one task that's feeling stuck and ask yourself, "What's missing?" Write down the first three things that come to mind and pick one to try immediately.

🎯 PUT IT INTO PRACTICE

Self-Talk: *I'm not failing. I'm just missing something, and I can fix that.*

One Small Action for Future You: Schedule a weekly 5-minute review where you scan your current projects and apply the "What's Missing?" lens proactively.

Reflection: What clue does your mind or body give you when you need to pause and reset?

Making the Clock Work for You

A guide to right-sizing your day, working with time blindness, and thinking beyond the to-do list

The other morning, I had what I thought was a quick 20-minute task. Send an email, add a couple of links, and move on. Ninety minutes later, I was still tinkering with it, and my carefully planned day was already in pieces.

If this sounds familiar, you know how draining it feels. You are not just behind schedule; you are behind in your own head. You replay the other things you "should" have done instead, and the pressure builds. The day feels shorter and heavier at the same time.

The truth is that time is simply harder to track when your brain does not naturally sense it. This is called time blindness. It can be frustrating, but it is not laziness. It is a difference in how your brain registers the passing minutes.

When you plan your days as if you have perfect time

awareness, you set yourself up to lose. When you design for the brain you actually have, the clock starts working *for* you instead of *against* you.

WHY THE CLOCK FEELS LIKE AN ENEMY

Time blindness means you have difficulty sensing how much time has passed or predicting how long something will take. It is tied to executive functioning skills such as:

- **Planning:** knowing the steps to take and when to take them
- **Time estimation:** predicting how long those steps will actually take
- **Task shifting:** moving between tasks without getting stuck or losing momentum

When those skills are under strain, it is easy to fall into the "where did the day go?" loop. The impact is not only practical but emotional. It can bring shame, constant rushing, and a nagging sense that you will never catch up.

If you have been living as if the clock is always winning, it is not because you are careless. You have been playing by rules that do not fit your brain.

SHRINK YOUR DAILY LIST TO REALITY

One of the fastest ways to lose to the clock is to write a fantasy schedule. If your daily list rarely gets finished, try the One-Third Rule:

- If you have written 15 tasks, pick 5.
- If you have written 9, pick 3.
- Put the rest on a "later" list.

Why It Works:
Fewer competing priorities mean a higher chance of completion. Finishing what you planned builds momentum. Your goals match your actual hours and energy. Partial credit counts too. Two-thirds of a task is still progress.

TRIPLE YOUR TIME ESTIMATES

If time always seems to disappear faster than you expect, try tripling your estimates.

- Writing an email that you think will take 5 minutes should be planned for 15.
- Cleaning the kitchen that you expect will take 20 minutes should be planned for 60.
- Creating a presentation that you expect will take 2 hours should be planned for 6.

This is not lowering the bar. It is removing the hidden pressure of unrealistic timelines and making space for:

- Steps your brain did not account for
- The inevitable interruptions
- The mental transition time between tasks

When you build in that buffer, you are more likely to finish what you start and less likely to feel like the day slipped away.

EXTERNALIZE THE PASSAGE OF TIME

If time does not naturally register for you, make it visible and tangible with tools like:

- Analog clocks that show the whole picture of how much time has passed and how much is left
- Visual timers you can check at a glance
- Vibrating watch timers that buzz periodically to pull your attention back to the clock

When time is externalized, you are less likely to lose an afternoon without realizing it. If you often lose track of time in a certain spot, such as while working at the kitchen table, put a clock right there. Solve the problem where it happens.

WORK WITH YOUR TIME HORIZONS

Some brains naturally live in "now" and "not now." That is okay, but zooming out can help. Try splitting your priorities into:

- **Today's Must-Dos:** things that absolutely have to happen today
- **This Week's Priorities:** important but not urgent
- **Future Self Projects:** ideas for later that do not need to clutter today's focus

This gives you a realistic picture of today without losing sight of the bigger picture.

CELEBRATE SMALL WINS

Your brain thrives on dopamine from success, so make sure you notice it. Try:

- Marking a task "done" when you have moved it forward, even if it is not finished
- Keeping a "done" list in your planner or notes app and reviewing it at the end of the day
- Sharing a win with someone so the progress sticks in your mind

When you replace the "I got nothing done" story with proof, you build the motivation to keep going.

WHY THIS MATTERS FOR NEURODIVERGENT BRAINS

Neurodivergent brains often struggle with accurate time estimation and remembering to check the clock, which can derail planning and progress. Externalizing time and adjusting expectations helps align your plans with how your brain actually experiences time, making follow-through more achievable and less stressful.

CLOSING GROUNDING TRUTH

You are not losing to the clock because you are lazy. You have been following time rules that do not fit your brain. When you shrink your list, stretch your timelines, externalize time, and celebrate your progress, you stop running out of time and start building time around you.

KEY TAKEAWAYS

Core Idea: Time blindness makes it harder to track and plan your day, but you can work with it instead of against it.

Big Shift: Instead of cramming more into the same hours, adjust timelines and task loads to match your actual energy and pace.

Practical Application: Use the One-Third List and Triple Your Time strategies to create realistic days and steady wins.

PUT IT INTO PRACTICE

Self-Talk: *I am not bad at time. I can plan for how my brain works.*

One Small Action for Future You: Cut tomorrow's list down by 2-thirds before you start the day.

Reflection: Picture yourself halfway through the day: What is the first sign, physical or mental, that tells you it is time to change course?

Prioritizing What Matters

Choosing what comes first when everything feels urgent

_____

WHEN EVERYTHING FEELS LIKE A FIRE

You sit down to start your day, and the list in front of you looks like a wall of flashing lights: Respond to emails. Prep for the meeting. Call the doctor. Fold the laundry before it piles higher. Pay that bill before the late fee hits. Each one whispers, *I'm urgent.*

If you're anything like me, the urge is to bounce from one thing to the next, hoping that if you move fast enough, you'll keep the whole ship afloat. But here's the trap: when everything feels urgent, nothing truly important rises to the top. You end up busy but not steady, moving but not satisfied.

WHY PRIORITIZING IS SO HARD

Prioritizing is not just about willpower. It's an executive function skill, and like all skills, it pulls on several mental processes at once. You have to weigh what matters most, estimate time and energy, and tolerate the discomfort of setting something aside. That's a lot of cognitive load.

Next, add in real-life pressures—deadlines at work, family needs, social expectations—and it's no wonder your brain throws up its hands and says, *Do it all. Do it now.*

And then, there's emotion. Choosing one thing means leaving something else undone, at least for now. That can trigger guilt, anxiety, or fear of disappointing others. Emotional regulation becomes part of the work of prioritizing.

So if you've ever felt stuck in the swirl, know this: It isn't laziness or lack of discipline. It's the complexity of a skill most people underestimate.

A Story You Might Recognize

I once worked with a client who described her mornings as "triage." She'd open her laptop, see 20 emails marked "urgent," glance at her calendar, remember her son's permission slip, and suddenly feel paralyzed. By the end of the day, she had answered most of the emails, half-finished the report, and was racing to the school drop-off bin at the last minute.

When we paused together and asked, "What actually matters most today?" she realized that 2 of those emails could wait, the report was the anchor task, and the permission slip could be handled in under 5 minutes if she just stopped spinning. With a little structure and self-permission to focus, the day shifted from reactive to intentional.

Shifting From Urgency to Importance

Here's the reframe: not everything deserves your top attention.

Urgent does not always mean important. The squeaky wheel may demand oil, but your long-term goals, health, and peace of mind also deserve a place on the list.

Sometimes, the most powerful act of prioritizing is asking, "What will actually matter tomorrow, next week, or next month?"

Gentle Tools to Try

- **Anchor Tasks:** Choose one or 2 things that, if finished today, will make you feel grounded. Everything else can orbit around those anchors.
- **The Eisenhower Lens:** Ask yourself: *Is this urgent? Is this important?* Some tasks are both, but many are only one or the other. The goal is to spend more time on the "important, not urgent" side of the things that move life forward before a crisis sets in.
- **Energy Matching:** Don't just ask *What matters most?* ask *What matters most given my energy right now?* Maybe the important project is best saved for your peak focus time, while small admin tasks can live in the afternoon slump.
- **Permission to De-Prioritize:** Sometimes the bravest choice is naming what won't get done

today. You're not failing; you're protecting space for what matters.

THINKING ABOUT YOUR FUTURE SELF

Future You doesn't need you to finish everything today. Future You needs clarity. A day with one meaningful task completed is more valuable than a day of half-finished flailing.

When you pause to choose, really choose, what deserves your attention now, you gift Future You less chaos, fewer emergencies, and more trust in your own ability to steer.

WHY THIS MATTERS FOR NEURODIVERGENT BRAINS

For people with executive functioning differences, prioritization isn't just about sorting tasks. It's about navigating time blindness, emotional intensity, and shifting energy levels. When you intentionally pause to choose what matters most, you free yourself from living only in reaction mode. This small shift builds confidence, follow-through, and momentum.

 KEY TAKEAWAYS

Core Idea: Prioritizing is an executive function skill that helps you choose what matters most when everything feels urgent.

Big Shift: Urgency is not the same as importance. Slowing down to choose prevents you from living in constant triage mode.

Practical Application: Use anchor tasks, energy matching, and permission to de-prioritize as tools for making daily choices.

🎯 PUT IT INTO PRACTICE

Self-Talk: *I can't do everything, but I can choose what matters most right now.*

One Small Action for Future You: Pick one anchor task today and give it your best attention. Let the rest fall into place around it.

Reflection: If you could finish only one thing today, which one would make Future You feel most supported?

When Tools Stop Working

Why even good strategies fade and what to do about it

_____

You have been using a visual timer every day for months. It sits on your desk like a trusty sidekick. It helps you focus, keeps you moving, and makes the day feel more manageable. Then one morning, you forget to set it. The next day, you tell yourself you will get to it later. Soon, it is buried under a pile of mail. You never decided to stop; it just quietly slipped out of your routine.

If this sounds familiar, you are not alone. Tools and systems that once worked brilliantly can fade without warning. It is not because you are inconsistent or bad at sticking to things. Your brain and your life are constantly changing. Even the best tools have a shelf life, and learning to work with that reality instead of against it can save you a lot of frustration.

Why Good Strategies Fade

The novelty effect wears off

ADHD brains especially thrive on the spark of newness. When that spark fades, so does the pull to keep using the tool. You forget, put it off, or stop noticing it.

Your season of life changes

What fit perfectly during one routine may not fit during another. A new job, shifting childcare needs, health changes, or a different environment can disrupt a system that once worked effortlessly.

The tool solved the problem

Sometimes, when the original challenge is resolved, the tool feels unnecessary. You stop using it until the problem creeps back in.

The tool became clutter

If keeping it going feels heavier than the benefit you get, your brain will naturally push it aside.

RECOGNIZING IT WITHOUT SHAME

Tool fade is not a sign you cannot commit. It is part of the natural cycle of using supports. The trick is noticing it early and responding without turning it into a character judgment.

Instead of spiraling into "I can never stick with anything," try reframing:

"This tool worked for me until it didn't. Now I know more about what I need."

Or remind yourself:

"I did not fail the tool. It served its purpose, and now I get to choose my next step."

Deciding What to Do Next

Option 1: Refresh It

Bring back the spark by changing the look, location, or method. Pair it with a new habit so it feels fresh again.

Example: I stopped noticing the sticky note reminders on my bathroom mirror. I replaced them with colorful index cards and rotated the messages weekly. Suddenly, they caught my eye again.

Option 2: Replace It

Sometimes, the core need is still there, but the delivery method needs to change. This is not abandoning a strategy; it is evolving it.

Example: I loved my magnetic fridge calendar until the kitchen remodel left me without wall space. I switched to a shared digital calendar that my family could access from their phones, and it kept the same function with a better fit for our new setup.

Option 3: Release It

If the tool is no longer needed, release it intentionally. Letting go is not giving up; it is making space for what fits now.

Example: I once tracked my water intake with a daily chart. Once drinking enough became automatic, the chart became busywork. I let it go without guilt.

Building a Flexible Mindset Around Tools

Expect tools to have a shelf life. When you accept this

as normal, you save yourself frustration.

- Make it a rhythm to check in quarterly. Ask: "Is this still helping?"
- Keep a "strategy list" of past wins so you can bring them back when life shifts.
- Put the support where the friction happens. If you forget to take your vitamins, put the bottle next to the coffee maker instead of in the pantry. Tools work best when they are in your daily path.

Why This Matters for Neurodivergent Brains

Neurodivergent brains often experience shifts in motivation and environment that make long-term consistency with a single tool unrealistic. Recognizing tool fade as normal allows you to adapt supports without shame, keeping systems effective as your needs and routines change.

 ## KEY TAKEAWAYS

Core Idea: Even the best tools have an expiration date. When they fade, it is feedback, not failure.

Big Shift: The goal is not to find one "forever" strategy but to keep evolving your supports as your life and brain change.

Practical Application: Regularly check your tools and systems. If one has faded, decide whether to refresh, replace, or release it without guilt.

 PUT IT INTO PRACTICE

Self-Talk: *This tool worked for me once, and it can again, or I can find something that works even better for this season.*

One Small Action for Future You: Pick one tool you have not used in weeks. Ask yourself if you want to refresh it, replace it, or release it, then act on that choice today.

Reflection: Which strategies from your past might be worth revisiting now that your life has shifted?

PART FOUR

DOING LIFE YOUR WAY

*Sustainable motivation, self-trust,
and redefining effort*

Progress Over Perfection (Every Time)

Start messy. Celebrate effort. Keep going.

You plan the perfect cleaning day. The playlist is ready, snacks are lined up, and your favorite cleaning supplies are within reach. But the morning gets derailed. You do nothing because you cannot do everything.

Perfectionism convinces you that "not perfect" is not worth doing. The result is a stalled start, mounting guilt, and the feeling that you have failed before you have begun.

WHY PERFECTIONISM TRIPS US UP

Perfectionism is not always about wanting things neat or beautiful. For many people with executive functioning challenges, it is about the mental rules we carry:

- **Executive Function Trap:** The bigger and more "ideal" the task, the harder it is to start.
- **All-or-Nothing Thinking:** If it is not perfect, it feels like it does not count.
- **Fear of Wasted Effort:** If it will not stay done,

why bother.
- **Comparison Brain:** Measuring yourself against someone else's highlight reel can lead to shame.

Perfectionism can take 2 main forms. Knowing which one shows up for you makes it easier to spot when it is stealing your momentum.

Front-End Perfectionism

This is when you get stuck before you even start. You plan and prepare endlessly, waiting for the "right" moment or the "perfect" conditions. You might spend hours researching the best cleaning method without ever picking up the sponge or tweaking your workout plan instead of doing the first rep. It feels productive, but it is really procrastination in disguise.

A friend of mine spent days re-reading her presentation notes, convinced she needed one more round of practice before presenting. She finally walked into the meeting still feeling unready and delivered it flawlessly. The extra days of stalling had changed nothing except her stress level.

Back-End Perfectionism

This shows up after you have started or even finished a task. You keep going over and over to refine, polish, and improve, long past the point of diminishing returns. You might rewrite a perfectly good email or spend an extra hour formatting a report that is already clear and complete. It is the voice that says "It is not ready yet" when it is more than ready enough.

Knowing When "Good Enough" Is Enough

Everything doesn't require your maximum effort. Deciding what "good enough" looks like before you start frees you from the perfectionism-procrastination loop.

Ask yourself:

- "What is the minimum needed to meet the goal of this task?"
- "What would "ideal" look like if I had unlimited time and energy?"
- "Where can I stop and still feel satisfied?"

Example: For a work report, the minimum might be "all required sections written and clear." The ideal might be "polished with perfect formatting." You might decide to set a 90-minute timer, get the content down, and call it complete when the time is up.

Sometimes "good enough" also means making your environment work for you. If a sink full of dishes feels overwhelming, you might place a small bin in the kitchen just for silverware, so at least one category gets handled easily. That small environmental shift can keep a task moving without relying on willpower alone.

Redefining Progress

Progress is not about flawless execution. It is anything that moves you forward, even an inch, such as:

- Washing 3 dishes instead of the whole sink
- Writing one paragraph instead of the entire report
- Walking to the mailbox instead of doing the full workout

One evening, I had planned to tidy the whole living room. By the time I got to it, my energy was gone. Instead of giving up, I cleared just the coffee table and put a load of laundry in the dryer. The next morning, that small pocket of order gave me momentum to finish the rest in 15 minutes.

Small wins stack. Every imperfect action you take is proof you are not stuck, and momentum feeds motivation.

THE MICRO-ACTION METHOD

Shrink the starting point until it feels almost too small to resist. For example:

- Five minutes of tidying
- The first sentence of an email
- One drawer instead of the whole kitchen

You have permission to stop after that first step, but often, you will not want to.

A client once wanted to start meditating daily but kept putting it off. We scaled it back to one deep breath before opening her laptop each morning. That single breath became 2 minutes of quiet time, then 5. Within weeks, she had the meditation habit she had been chasing for years by starting with almost nothing.

CELEBRATING IMPERFECT EFFORT

It is easy to skip over small actions because they do not match your ideal picture. But those actions matter. Keep a "done list" or progress journal so you can see your forward motion in black and white.

- Swap "I only..." for "I started"
- Swap "It is not finished" for "It is further along than before"

Completion, even in rough form, lightens your mental load and builds confidence.

PROTECTING PROGRESS WITH GENTLE BOUNDARIES

- Do not let perfect plans ruin good-enough actions.
- Drop "restart rules" that require perfection to resume (no more "I will start again on Monday").
- Make progress part of your identity: "I am someone who keeps moving, even in tiny ways."

WHY THIS MATTERS FOR NEURODIVERGENT BRAINS

Neurodivergent brains often have difficulty starting or finishing tasks when perfectionism sets unrealistic standards. Learning to define "good enough" and celebrate imperfect progress supports initiation, follow-through, and the ability to build sustainable momentum.

 KEY TAKEAWAYS

Core Idea: Perfectionism is a momentum killer. Progress, in any form, is the goal.

Big Shift: Imperfect action is not less; it is often the only way to keep going.

Practical Application: Decide on "good enough" before you start, and shrink your starting point until it is easy enough to begin.

PUT IT INTO PRACTICE

Self-Talk: *I am moving forward, and that counts.*

One Small Action for Future You: Pick one stalled task and cut it down to the smallest possible step you can take today.

Reflection: If you woke up tomorrow and perfectionism was not in the way, what is the first small thing you would notice yourself doing differently?

Worth Doing Messy

Why clumsy, real effort moves you forward

_____

One of the biggest lies productivity culture sells us is that things only count if they are done fully, neatly, and all at once. If you cannot do it perfectly, you may as well not do it at all.

But here is the truth: almost everything is worth doing messy, clumsy, and real.

I see this with clients all the time. Someone sets out to go to the gym for a 45-minute workout. That is their "ideal." But on the days when energy is low or time disappears, the choice becomes all or nothing: go all in or not at all. That is where I encourage them to reset their zero. Instead of saying "either 45 minutes or nothing," we create a backup plan: a 7-minute workout video, a 5-minute stretch, or even one lap around the block.

Better than zero. Messy, clumsy, but real.

That small shift keeps you moving. It reinforces the rhythm and identity of "I am someone who takes care of my body" without demanding perfection every time. Over weeks and months, those better-than-zero efforts add up to far more than nothing.

Why Messy Matters

Messy action cuts through executive functioning friction. When you give yourself permission to do something imperfectly you:

- Lower the activation energy to start
- Bypass the shame of "I failed because I did not do it right"
- Build momentum you can carry into tomorrow

Think about it: A sink half-emptied is easier to face than one left untouched. A half-drafted email keeps the thread alive. A short stretch reminds your body that you care for it, even if it was not the full workout you planned.

Messy action is often the bridge between "stuck" and "done enough."

Resetting Zero in Daily Life

Resetting zero means defining a minimum version of a task that still counts. Not the perfect version, not the all-or-nothing version, just a better-than-nothing version.

Examples:
- **Laundry:** Toss in one load, even if folding waits until tomorrow

- **Meals:** Make toast with peanut butter instead of cooking a full dinner
- **Work:** Write 2 messy bullet points when a polished draft feels impossible
- **Home:** Clear just the coffee table when the whole room feels overwhelming

One client used to stall on grocery shopping because planning full meals felt too big. Their better-than-zero became grabbing a rotisserie chicken and pre-cut vegetables. Was it fancy? No. But it fed their family and stopped the cycle of takeout followed by guilt.

Another client's weekly goal was to keep up with emails. Their reset zero was replying to just one flagged message before logging off. On the nights when they had nothing left, that single reply kept the inbox from snowballing into overwhelm.

One parent I worked with used better-than-zero for house cleaning. They set a 5-minute timer to pick up toys. Sometimes the timer went off, and they stopped. Other times, 5 minutes rolled into 15. Either way, the house was lighter, and so was their mental load.

The key is to make your "zero" flexible enough that you can always do something—no matter how small.

THE RIPPLE EFFECT OF BETTER THAN ZERO

When you reset zero, you give yourself a realistic baseline to return to. That baseline keeps you from slipping into long stretches of doing nothing, which are much harder to climb out of later.

One client told me their better-than-zero for journaling was a single sentence. Some nights, that was all they wrote. Other nights, that one sentence unlocked a whole page. But no matter what, they gave themselves credit.

Another client set their better-than-zero for housework as a 5-minute kitchen reset. Even if the counters were not spotless, they went to bed with fewer dishes in the sink. Over time, that habit shifted the feel of their home. Not perfectly tidy, but far less overwhelming.

This is the power of messy effort. It keeps you out of shame. It keeps momentum alive. It gives your future self a head start.

GENTLE SELF-TALK FOR MESSY ACTION

When perfectionism pushes back, try these reframes:

- "I am not lowering the bar; I am keeping myself in motion."
- "Done clumsy is still done."
- "This is better than zero, and better than zero counts."

Permission to be messy is permission to keep going.

WHY THIS MATTERS FOR NEURODIVERGENT BRAINS

ADHD and executive functioning challenges magnify the all-or-nothing trap. If you believe you need the full plan, the perfect focus, or the "right" energy before starting, you will stall out. Resetting zero reframes success as incremental, approachable, and sustainable. That is what makes follow-through possible over time.

Your brain does not need the pressure of perfect. It needs the relief of knowing there is always a next step, no matter how small.

Closing Grounding Truth

Life rarely gives us ideal conditions. But progress does not need to be perfect. The smallest, messiest effort is still progress, and progress stacks. Every time you choose better-than-zero, you are proving to yourself that you do not have to wait for perfect to move forward.

 KEY TAKEAWAYS

Core Idea: Messy, clumsy action is still worthwhile; it keeps you in motion.

Big Shift: Redefine "success" as better than zero, not all-or-nothing.

Practical Application: Pick one habit and test a minimal version today to see if it's doable on a tough day.

⌖ PUT IT INTO PRACTICE

Self-Talk: *I can reset my zero and still move forward.*

One Small Action for Future You: Reflect on a habit that frequently stalls and plan a "better-than-zero" version that reduces guilt and keeps momentum in the long term.

Reflection: What's one area of life where you've been waiting for perfect conditions, and what would your messy, clumsy, better-than-zero version look like?

Mindfulness and Mono-Tasking

Paying attention on purpose and the power of one-thing-at-a-time

---

ATTENTION AS THE REAL RESOURCE

We live in a world that constantly asks for more than one thing at a time. Notifications ping, kids call from the next room, a colleague drops in with a "quick question." Your brain tries to keep up, juggling tasks and shifting attention in rapid-fire bursts. It looks like productivity, but in reality, it often leaves you scattered and drained.

For adults with executive functioning challenges, this pressure to multitask hits especially hard. Working memory gets overloaded, transitions pile up, and focus splinters. That's why mindfulness—the practice of paying attention on purpose and without judgment—can be such a powerful antidote.

Mindfulness doesn't have to mean sitting still for 30 minutes in silence. At its core, it's simply the skill of noticing the present moment with curiosity. It's catching yourself when your attention drifts and choosing, gently, to come back. It's remembering that one-thing-at-a-time is not a weakness but a strength.

Why Mindfulness Matters for Executive Functioning

Executive functioning depends on your ability to notice and direct your attention. When attention is scattered, everything else becomes harder—planning, prioritizing, starting tasks, and even regulating emotions.

Mindfulness strengthens those skills. It trains you to catch distraction, to pause before reacting, and to anchor yourself long enough to follow through. It's also one of the most practical tools for emotional regulation. Instead of getting swept up in frustration, worry, or reactivity, mindfulness creates a small pause where you can notice the feeling, let it move through, and choose how to respond.

Attention is also the gateway to memory. If your mind isn't present when something happens, your brain can't capture it in the first place. That's why we misplace our keys or forget details from conversations; we weren't truly there when the information passed by. Practicing mindfulness opens the gate so your brain can store details long enough to use them later.

The Power of Mono-Tasking

If mindfulness is the *how* of attention, mono-tasking is the *what*. Mono-tasking means doing one thing at a time, fully, instead of scattering focus across 3 or 4 things at once.

In practice, mono-tasking might look like eating lunch without scrolling on your phone, writing an email without bouncing to another tab, or listening to your child's story without running your to-do list in your head.

It sounds simple, but in a culture that praises multi-tasking, mono-tasking can feel almost rebellious. And yet, when you allow your brain to settle on one thing, tasks often take less time, feel less overwhelming, and leave you with more energy.

Everyday Mindfulness: No Extra Time Required

You don't need to carve out hours to practice mindfulness. The ordinary routines of your day can become training grounds for focus.

Instead of brushing your teeth while mentally rehearsing tomorrow's meeting, notice the taste of the toothpaste and the rhythm of the brush. Instead of rushing through dishes, notice the warmth of the water and the clink of the plates. When you walk outside, feel your feet on the ground and the air on your face.

Even conversations can become a mindfulness practice. Focus on the person in front of you, notice their tone and expression. When your mind drifts to what you'll say next, gently bring it back to listening.

You're not adding new tasks; you're doing the same ones with a different kind of attention.

CHECKING IN WITH YOUR SENSORY WORLD

One way to bring yourself back into the moment is by checking in with your senses. Your environment shapes focus more than you realize.

- **Sight:** Look around. Is your space calm or cluttered? Clear one small thing.
- **Sound:** Notice what you hear. Lower distracting noise or add sounds to support focus.
- **Touch:** Adjust your chair, your clothing, or even hold a grounding object.
- **Smell and Taste:** Light a candle, sip tea, or open a window—small cues that reset your brain.

Your senses are levers you can pull to make attention easier, especially when your mind feels scattered.

TRAINING YOUR ATTENTION LIKE A MUSCLE

Attention works like a muscle. The more you practice, the stronger it gets. You wouldn't walk into a gym and lift the heaviest weight on day one. Focus works the same way; small stretches build strength over time.

Start by noticing your current baseline. How long can you focus before your mind wanders? Two minutes? Five? That's your starting point. Then, set a gentle target, just a little longer. Choose an anchor, a breath, a sound, or the task itself. Each time your mind drifts, notice it and come back.

And here's something important: sometimes, what pulls your attention isn't noise outside but thoughts inside—worries, judgments, or "what ifs." Mindfulness teaches you to notice those thoughts without climbing onto them. You can picture them as clouds drifting past or cars passing on the road. You don't have to chase every one. You can let them go and return to what you choose instead.

You're not failing when your mind wanders. You're strengthening your attention every time you return.

A WORD ABOUT MEDITATION

When people hear "mindfulness," they often picture meditation—sitting quietly, focusing on the breath. Meditation can be powerful, but it isn't the only way. Mindfulness can happen while washing dishes, during a walk, or even in the middle of work.

If stillness feels uncomfortable, movement can become your practice. The method matters less than the act of noticing.

WHY THIS MATTERS FOR NEURODIVERGENT BRAINS

For people with executive functioning differences, paying attention on purpose is more than self-care; it's a foundation. It reduces overwhelm, makes follow-through more likely, and builds confidence in your ability to steer your own brain.

Mindfulness and mono-tasking create margin in a world that constantly pulls you in every direction. They remind you that attention is yours to direct, not something you have to surrender to every ping or distraction.

Thinking About Your Future Self

Future You doesn't need a longer to-do list. Future You needs the capacity to focus on what matters in the moment. By practicing mindfulness and choosing mono-tasking, you give Future You more energy, fewer mistakes to clean up, and a deeper sense of presence in daily life.

The One-Task Challenge

For one day, choose a single routine activity, such as making coffee, eating a meal, or folding laundry, and commit to doing it without multitasking. No phone, no side conversations, no rushing ahead. Just one thing, start to finish.

Notice how it feels. Does time slow down? Do you feel calmer, more focused, or less scattered? That one-task practice is the essence of mindfulness in daily life: attention on purpose, grounded in the present, creating relief instead of overwhelm.

 **KEY TAKEAWAYS**

Core Idea: Mindfulness and mono-tasking strengthen the foundation of executive functioning.

Big Shift: Attention isn't automatic; it's a skill you can practice. One-thing-at-a-time is not failure; it's focus.

Practical Application: Pick one routine today and give it your full attention from start to finish, noticing any distractions or thoughts that arise.

🎯 PUT IT INTO PRACTICE

Self-Talk: *I don't have to do everything at once. I can give this one thing my full attention.*

One Small Action for Future You: Identify one everyday action (like brushing your teeth or making coffee) and create a daily mindfulness routine around it going forward.

Reflection: Where in your day would one-thing-at-a-time feel like relief instead of restriction?

Creating Space for Transitions

How to soften the edges between tasks and roles

WHY TRANSITIONS FEEL SO HARD

Most people underestimate how much energy it takes to move from one task to the next. It's not just the task itself that drains us; it's the shifting in between.

Transitions are the moments when you're switching gears—leaving work and stepping into home life, wrapping up dinner to begin bedtime routines, moving from answering emails to focusing on deep work. For many adults with executive functioning challenges, those edges feel sharp. The brain lingers on the last thing while being pulled toward the next, leaving you stuck in the middle.

You may notice it in small ways, wandering around instead of starting the next task, scrolling your phone to buffer the shift, or avoiding the new thing altogether. It's not procrastination so much as your brain needing time to switch tracks.

What's Really Going On

Executive functioning is what allows you to shift attention, reset your emotional state, and pick up new information. That takes cognitive effort. When your brain is already taxed, transitions can feel like hitting a speed bump over and over again.

Sometimes the challenge is task inertia; your brain is still in motion from the previous task and resists starting the next one. Other times, it's cognitive residue; your mind replays what just happened while you're supposed to be moving on. Transitions can also carry an emotional load. Stress from one role (like work) bleeds into another (like family), leaving you reactive in ways that don't fit the new context. Add in decision fatigue—the dozens of tiny choices required to switch gears—and it's no wonder transitions feel sticky.

When you see them this way, it becomes clear: Struggling with transitions isn't laziness. It's the predictable friction of an overloaded system.

Creating Space as a Strategy

The good news is transitions don't have to feel like whiplash. By creating intentional space between tasks and roles, you give your brain the buffer it needs to reset. Think of it as softening the edges.

That space can be tiny—just a minute or 2—or longer if you have it. The goal isn't more downtime; it's purposeful downtime. Think of it as space that clears mental residue, signals closure, and prepares you for what's next.

Micro-Transitions: Small Shifts Help

You don't need elaborate rituals. Even the simplest actions can create the separation your brain craves.

- **Physical Reset:** Stand up, stretch, or walk into a different room. Movement cues your brain that one chapter has ended and another has begun.
- **Sensory Reset:** Wash your hands, light a candle, change the lighting, or sip a glass of water. Small sensory shifts mark the change.
- **Environmental Reset:** Tidy your desk, close your laptop, or clear one surface. Your surroundings reinforce the new start.
- **Breath Reset:** Take one deep inhale and exhale or a 2-minute pause with your eyes closed. Quick grounding rituals calm your nervous system.

These resets act like bookends. They don't take long, but they give structure to the in-between.

Bigger Transitions: Routines Between Roles

Some transitions are more significant, like leaving work mode for family time or wrapping up a busy day before bedtime. These call for routines that act like bridges.

- **End-of-Work Ritual:** Shut down your computer, write tomorrow's top 3 tasks, and close the office door (even if it's just a laptop

on the kitchen table).
- **Family Arrival Ritual:** Change clothes, put your phone away, or share a quick check-in with loved ones before diving into dinner or chores.
- **Bedtime Ritual:** Lower lights, stack tomorrow's essentials (keys, bag, lunch), and use calming cues like tea, reading, or soft music.

When practiced consistently, these rituals teach your brain to let go of one role and enter another with less friction.

WHY THIS MATTERS FOR ENERGY

Transitions aren't wasted time; they're energy management in disguise. Without them, you burn more fuel pushing through cognitive and emotional friction. With them, you arrive fresher and more focused for what comes next.

Think of it like driving: constant stop-and-go traffic burns gas quickly, while steady cruising preserves it. Transitions are your chance to slow down and shift gears before accelerating again.

A STORY YOU MIGHT RECOGNIZE

Imagine finishing a work call and immediately trying to jump into family dinner prep. Your mind is still replaying the meeting while your kids ask questions and the pasta boils over. The result: stress, mistakes, and snapping at the people you love.

Now picture the same moment with a 2-minute

transition. You end the call, jot down one follow-up note, then step outside for a deep breath. When you walk back in, you're more grounded and present. Dinner prep is still busy, but the edges feel softer.

Same tasks, different energy, because you created space.

A Transition Menu

Think of this as a grab-and-go list. You don't need to invent a new ritual every time. You can simply choose one from your menu and let it signal the shift.

- One deep breath with eyes closed
- Stretch or change posture
- Wash your hands or splash cool water on your face
- Step outside for 30 seconds of fresh air
- Write down one "done" from the last task and one "next" for the new one
- Change the lighting or put on different music
- Swap environments (move from desk to couch, from kitchen to bedroom)

Keep it simple. The point isn't to do all of these; it's to have options ready so you don't default to scrolling or stalling.

Thinking About Your Future Self

Future You doesn't need you to power through every transition. They need a buffer that protects your energy, focus, and relationships. Creating small rituals now spares Future You the stress of sharp edges later.

WHY THIS MATTERS FOR NEURODIVERGENT BRAINS

For many neurodivergent adults, transitions can be the hardest part of the day. It's not the tasks themselves but the shifting. By externalizing and ritualizing transitions, you reduce the invisible load on your executive functions. Instead of burning energy on friction, you free it up for follow-through.

 ## KEY TAKEAWAYS

Core Idea: Transitions are where much of the friction of daily life hides.

Big Shift: Create space between tasks and roles to soften the edges and reduce overwhelm.

Practical Application: Try one option from the Transition Menu today and see how it changes the feel of your next shift.

 ## PUT IT INTO PRACTICE

Self-Talk: *I'm not stalling. I'm giving my brain space to reset.*

One Small Action for Future You: Before your next transition, pause for one minute. Close your eyes, breathe, and let the last task go.

Reflection: Where in your day do transitions feel sharpest? What would it look like to soften the edge with a simple ritual?

Breaking the Avoidance–Urgency Cycle

Why last-minute pressure feels motivating and how to break free

---

Why We Wait Until the Last Minute

Have you ever noticed that the less you want to do something, the longer you put it off until the deadline is breathing down your neck? And then, suddenly, the task gets done in a rush of stress and adrenaline. That temporary flood of urgency can feel like magic, but it usually leaves exhaustion, guilt, and the promise that "next time" will be different.

This is the avoidance–urgency cycle, and it's one of the most common and most draining patterns for people with executive functioning challenges. Tasks don't get done because they're easy; they get done because crisis makes them impossible to avoid. The relief is real, but so is the cost.

What's Really Happening Beneath the Cycle

It's tempting to frame this pattern as procrastination or poor discipline, but the roots are deeper. Several factors collide to make last-minute pressure feel so powerful, such as:

- **Time blindness** makes it hard to sense how much time has passed or how much is left. Deadlines sneak up, and urgency becomes the only clock that sticks.
- **Emotional avoidance** creeps in when a task feels boring, overwhelming, or tied to self-doubt. Avoiding the task buys temporary relief but builds long-term stress.
- **Stimulation needs** mean that the adrenaline of urgency finally provides the jolt of motivation the brain has been craving.
- **Perfectionism** raises the bar so high that starting early feels impossible. If it can't be perfect, better to avoid until you can't anymore.
- **Executive function load** makes task initiation, planning, and sequencing heavy work for the brain. Crisis clears the clutter because it forces a singular focus.

Seen this way, the cycle isn't laziness. It's a brain trying to cope with a mismatch between its wiring and its environment.

WHY URGENCY FEELS LIKE IT WORKS

Here's the tricky part: urgency *does* work, at least temporarily.

The looming deadline delivers adrenaline, and

adrenaline delivers focus. Many people even describe themselves as doing their "best work" under pressure. But this is survival mode, not sustainable productivity.

Living in crisis carries hidden costs like frayed relationships, diminished quality of work, chronic stress, and a nervous system always braced for impact. The cycle keeps tasks moving, but it drains the person carrying them.

Naming the Loop Without Shame

The first step in breaking the cycle is simply noticing it. Shame only adds weight and makes starting harder. Try saying, "I see that I am in the avoidance-urgency loop right now." That small act of naming creates space between you and the behavior. You are not the loop. You are a person whose brain sometimes leans on urgency for fuel.

Shifting the Pattern in Gentle Ways

Breaking free doesn't mean never feeling urgency again. It means experimenting with ways to lower avoidance and invite motivation earlier.

Start ridiculously small. Instead of "write the report," try "open the document and type the title." Instead of "clean the kitchen," try "put one plate in the dishwasher." When you shrink the entry point, you remove the weight of perfectionism and give your brain a quick hit of progress.

Borrow external supports. Time is slippery, so make

it visible. Use timers, alarms, or visual clocks. Work alongside someone else, even virtually, so you don't have to generate momentum alone. Offloading these demands frees your brain to focus on the task itself.

Create urgency without the crisis. If urgency motivates you, build it in earlier. Share a self-imposed deadline with a colleague or friend. Turn a task into a race against your tea cooling down. Use apps or games that reward progress. Urgency can be useful fuel, but it doesn't have to wait until the last possible second.

Address the feelings under avoidance. Often, it's not the task itself but the emotions attached to it. Fear of failure, boredom, or vulnerability can all make avoidance feel safer. Ask yourself: *What feeling am I dodging right now?* Then try one small adjustment: pair the task with music, give yourself permission for a "rough draft," or ask for help.

Redefine what counts. The cycle thrives on all-or-nothing thinking. Either the whole task is done perfectly, or it doesn't get touched. But what if success was just one step forward? Momentum builds faster when progress, not perfection, is the measure.

Protect your energy. Sometimes, avoidance shows up because you're depleted. Breaks that restore—walking outside, stretching, music, or quiet—aren't wasted time. They refill the fuel tank so you don't rely on panic for momentum.

A Story You Might Recognize

You put off working on a big report for weeks. The night before the deadline, adrenaline kicks in and you power through until 2am. The report gets submitted, mission accomplished, but the cost is exhaustion, stress, and a next-day fog that makes everything else harder.

Now picture a different approach. On day one, you spend 5 minutes jotting down the main points. On day 2, you write a rough, messy first section without worrying about polish. By day 3, you schedule a short co-working session with a colleague or set a timer to keep yourself moving. The report still takes effort, but the work is spread out, the stress is lighter, and you finish feeling capable instead of drained.

Same brain, same task. Different approach.

Thinking About Your Future Self

Future You doesn't want every task to arrive with sirens blaring. Future You wants to trust that things can move forward without panic. Each time you start earlier, even in the smallest way, you send Future You a message: *I can do this without the fire drill.*

Why This Matters for Neurodivergent Brains

The avoidance–urgency cycle often shows up in neuro-divergent adults not because of laziness, but because of how motivation, time, and emotions are processed differently. Naming the cycle, removing shame, and experimenting with brain-friendly supports creates freedom. It's not about "fixing procrastination," it's about building patterns that honor how your brain works while reducing the toll of constant crisis.

 ## KEY TAKEAWAYS

Core Idea: The avoidance–urgency cycle keeps tasks moving but at a steep cost.

Big Shift: Urgency isn't the only source of motivation; you can create momentum earlier with gentler strategies.

Practical Application: Pick one small experiment this week—like starting a task with a 2-minute timer or asking a friend to be your accountability partner—and notice how it changes the feel of the work.

PUT IT INTO PRACTICE

Self-Talk: *Urgency doesn't have to be my only fuel. I can start small.*

One Small Action for Future You: Choose one task and set a playful mini-deadline (i.e., before the tea cools, before the song ends, before the top of the hour).

Reflection: What's one sign that tells you you're in the avoidance–urgency loop? What would it look like to interrupt it earlier?

Process vs. Outcome Practices

Shifting focus from results to actions you can control

WHY THE FINISH LINE ISN'T ALWAYS THE POINT

Think about the last time you set a big intention. Maybe it was to finish a project at work, run a 5K, declutter your whole house, or finally get your finances in order. Chances are, you pictured the finish line, the report submitted, the medal around your neck, the sparkling clean kitchen, the debt finally paid off.

That picture of success can feel motivating in the moment. But if you've ever felt discouraged when the finish line seemed too far away or given up altogether because the results didn't come fast enough, you're not alone.

For adults with executive functioning challenges, out-come practices can feel especially slippery. You want the result, but the path to get there often feels unclear, overwhelming, or too long. That's where process prac-tices come in. Instead of pinning your hope on the finish line, process practices shift the focus to the steps you take along the way, the daily or weekly actions you can actually control.

A Story You Might Recognize

I once coached a client who wanted to "be more organized." That was her big outcome practice. But every time she looked around at the piles of papers, the full email inbox, and the clutter in her office, the gap between where she was and where she wanted to be felt impossible. She'd start strong—buying bins, downloading apps, making color-coded plans—but the momentum always fizzled.

When we reframed her practice as a process, everything changed. Instead of "get organized," her process practice became "spend 10 minutes at the end of each workday putting things back in their place." That one small action didn't magically clean her office overnight. But it built consistency, trust, and momentum. Over time, the office shifted. More importantly, she shifted from someone who felt constantly behind to someone who trusted her own follow-through.

The Difference Between Outcome and Process

Let's name the difference clearly:

- **Outcome practices** are the results you want to achieve. They're the finish lines: publish the book, lose 10 pounds, pay off debt, land the promotion.
- **Process practices** are the actions you commit to along the way. They're the training runs, the

writing sessions, the budgeting check-ins, the practice conversations.

Outcome practices answer the question: *What do I want?*

Process practices answer the question: *What will I actually do?*

Both matter. Outcome practices give direction and vision. But process practices are where progress actually happens.

Why Outcome Practices Can Backfire

For people with executive functioning challenges, outcome practices often trip us up for a few reasons:

- **They feel too far away.** When the finish line is months or years down the road, motivation fizzles.
- **They create pressure.** Focusing only on the result makes every stumble feel like failure.
- **They depend on variables outside your control.** You can write the book, but you can't control whether it becomes a bestseller. You can apply for the job, but you can't control who else is interviewing.
- **They feed all-or-nothing thinking.** Either you hit the target or you don't—there's little room to celebrate the steps along the way.

This doesn't mean outcome practices are bad. It just

means they're incomplete.

Why Process Practices Work Better

Process practices are smaller, repeatable, and within your control. They take motivation out of the abstract and put it into motion.

- **They shrink overwhelm.** "Clean the garage" is overwhelming. "Take one box off the shelf and sort it" feels doable.
- **They build consistency.** You may not see results immediately, but repeating a process creates progress over time.
- **They boost confidence.** Each small win proves to your brain that you can start, act, and finish.
- **They create momentum.** Even messy, imperfect action moves you closer to the outcome than staying frozen in dread.

A Practical Example

Let's say your outcome practice is to run a 5K.

- **Outcome:** Cross the finish line of a 5K race in June.
- **Process:** Run 3 times a week for 20 minutes, gradually increasing distance.

The process practice doesn't guarantee you'll win the race or even love running. But it guarantees you'll show up, build stamina, and increase your chances of crossing the finish line.

Imagine your outcome practice is to "be less over-whelmed at work." That's vague and hard to measure. A process practice might be: "Start each morning by writing down 3 priorities before opening email." That one shift doesn't fix everything, but it creates a rhythm of focus that can ripple outward.

Making Peace With Results

Here's the counterintuitive part: when you focus on the process, the outcomes often take care of themselves.

Instead of obsessing over whether you've lost 10 pounds, you focus on cooking 3 balanced meals a week. Instead of stressing over the promotion, you focus on delivering one clear update in each meeting. The outcomes may still come, but even if they don't, you've gained habits, confidence, and progress that matter on their own.

Process practices also protect your self-worth. When you hang all your value on whether you hit the big out-come, disappointment can sting deeply. But when you celebrate process wins, you always have something to be proud of: *I showed up. I did the thing. That counts.*

Thinking About Your Future Self

Future You doesn't just want the medal, the book, or the clean garage. Future You needs systems that make showing up easier, not just once but again and again.

When you focus on process practices, you're building scaffolding for Future You:

- A routine that makes the next step automatic
- A habit that carries you even on low-energy days
- A foundation of trust that says, *I can count on myself to take action, even when motivation is thin*

That's the real gift.

WHY THIS MATTERS FOR NEURODIVERGENT BRAINS

For people with executive functioning differences, starting is often the hardest part. Outcome practices can keep you stuck at the starting line, staring at how far away the finish seems. Process practices flip the script. They break the big thing into pieces small enough to begin.

And because process practices focus on actions within your control, they reduce the emotional weight of perfectionism. You don't have to control the whole outcome. You just have to take the next step.

 ## KEY TAKEAWAYS

Core Idea: Outcome practices define the destination, but process practices create the path.

Big Shift: Results may be outside your control, but actions are not. Focusing on process makes progress possible.

Practical Application: Pick a goal this week and turn it into a single, repeatable process step today, noticing progress instead of results (e.g., "15 minutes on one drawer" instead of "declutter the whole house").

🎯 PUT IT INTO PRACTICE

Self-Talk: *I don't have to finish today. I just have to take the next step.*

One Small Action for Future You: Choose a larger goal you've been stuck on and create a daily process habit that moves you forward automatically, reducing overwhelm and "all-or-nothing" pressure.

Reflection: If I measured my success by the actions I took, not just the results I achieved, what would I already be proud of?

Crossing the Finish Line

Why closure matters more than perfection, and how to follow through

---

THE STRUGGLE TO FINISH

Starting can be hard, but finishing has its own kind of weight. How many projects have you begun with excitement only to leave half-done: a report waiting for edits, a craft project in a box, a course with only 2 modules left?

There's often relief in starting and energy in the middle, but the finish line brings pressure. Suddenly, perfectionism creeps in: *If I finish this, people will see it. If I call it done, it can be judged.* Or avoidance takes over: *I'll come back later when I have more time, more energy, more clarity.*

The truth is, leaving things open drains you. Every unfinished task lingers in the background like a tab left open on your computer, quietly consuming bandwidth. Closure matters not because you need to finish everything perfectly, but because crossing the finish line frees your brain to move forward.

A STORY YOU MIGHT RECOGNIZE

One client told me about a big presentation she had to prepare. She built the slides, collected all the data, and had the deck 90% finished. But then she noticed little formatting issues and slides she wanted to polish. She told herself she would "fix it before sending it out." Days went by. The deadline passed, and she ended up scrambling with last-minute stress instead of sharing the solid work she already had.

What stopped her wasn't the task; it was the fear of imperfection. That presentation, which could have showcased her expertise, turned into a source of guilt. Later, when she finally shared her draft version in another meeting, her colleagues were impressed. They didn't notice the uneven fonts or slightly messy graphs. What mattered was that the ideas were communicated clearly.

Finishing is rarely about flawless results. It's about creating momentum and offering value, even if it isn't perfect.

WHY FINISHING IS HARD FOR EXECUTIVE FUNCTIONING

Executive functioning skills are the behind-the-scenes tools that carry you to the finish line: planning, organization, sustained attention, and self-monitoring. But these are also the very skills that can lag when you're tired, stressed, or neurodivergent.

Here's what often gets in the way:

- **Task initiation flips into task completion struggles.** Starting takes effort, but so does pushing through the last 10%.
- **Perfectionism hijacks closure.** If it can't be flawless, it's better to wait, fix, or abandon it.
- **Sustained attention fizzles.** The energy of novelty fades, and the boring details remain.
- **Planning gaps appear.** You didn't map out the final steps, so the ending feels bigger than it is.
- **Follow-through feels less rewarding.** Once the exciting part is over, finishing can feel anticlimactic compared to starting.

Understanding these barriers isn't an excuse; it's clarity. It helps you see why you stall, so you can make the finish line easier to cross.

Why Closure Matters More Than Perfection

Finishing brings closure. Closure means you can set something down, free your brain from the mental tab, and create space for the next thing. Without closure, everything lingers in limbo, pulling energy, focus, and self-trust.

And closure builds confidence. Each time you follow through, you teach your brain: *I can finish. I can count on myself.* That self-trust matters more than whether the final product is flawless.

The paradox is that finished usually matters more than flawless. The report with rough edges still lands on your manager's desk. The email that is short and simple still clears up confusion. The text that is a little clumsy still lets your friend know you care. What matters most is the closure and the connection, not the polish.

A Different Definition of Finishing

Part of what makes finishing hard is that we define it too narrowly. Finishing doesn't always mean every box is checked or every detail is wrapped with a bow. Sometimes, finishing is:

- Submitting the project at "good enough"
- Declaring a hobby project complete, even if it isn't gallery-ready
- Calling a space decluttered enough to function
- Ending a meeting with clear next steps instead of waiting for perfect consensus

Finishing is about calling something closed, not flawless.

Tools for Following Through

1. Break the Finish Line Into Steps

Sometimes, the final 10% feels harder than the first 90%. Instead of "finish the project," write down the last 2 or 3 specific steps. For example:

- Draft complete → proofread once → send
- Slides created → add speaker notes → share with team

When you see the end as small actions, it feels lighter.

2. Use "Done for Now" Language

If perfectionism is the barrier, practice saying, *This is done for now.* You can always revisit later, but calling it complete in this moment gives you closure and frees your brain.

3. Shrink Your Standards

Ask: "What would 80% finished look like? What if good enough was truly enough?" Many times, that's all anyone needs.

4. Create External Accountability

Tell someone: "I'll send you the draft by Thursday." Or set a timer and promise yourself you'll wrap up in that window. Deadlines don't have to be scary; they can be supportive nudges.

5. Celebrate the Finish

Don't rush past the ending. Pause, mark it, and celebrate—even with something as small as saying out loud, *That's done.* Celebration wires your brain to feel reward in closure, not just in starting.

THINKING ABOUT YOUR FUTURE SELF

Future You doesn't need a pile of half-finished projects that whisper guilt every time you see them. Future You needs closure, rooms you can use, projects that are off your mind, tasks that are truly behind you.

When you finish, even imperfectly, you give Future You relief. You reduce the clutter, not just physically but mentally. You teach Future You that things don't have to drag forever; they can be resolved, checked off, and put to rest.

WHY THIS MATTERS FOR NEURODIVERGENT BRAINS

For adults with executive functioning differences, the struggle to finish can feed a painful story: *I never follow through. I always drop the ball.* That story erodes confidence and makes starting even harder next time.

But when you practice finishing—messily, imperfectly, "done for now"—you rewrite that story. You prove to yourself that follow-through is possible. You begin to build momentum that doesn't rely on perfection, just on closure.

 KEY TAKEAWAYS

Core Idea: Closure matters more than perfection. Finishing frees your brain to move forward.

Big Shift: Done doesn't mean flawless; it means closed, complete for now, and off your plate.

Practical Application: Break your finish line into 2–3 final steps and aim for "done for now" instead of "done forever."

🎯 PUT IT INTO PRACTICE

Self-Talk: *Finishing imperfectly still counts. Closure is more powerful than polish.*

One Small Action for Future You: Pick one task that's 90% complete and take the last step, send the email, tie up the loose end, or declare it done for now.

Reflection: How would it feel to walk into tomorrow without this unfinished thing weighing on you?

Small Shifts, Big Impact

The surprising power of micro-decisions

_____

You swap your phone for a book on your nightstand. You only read for 5 minutes before bed, but after a week, you have read more than you have in months.

It did not feel like much in the moment, just a tiny choice, but it snowballed into a change you had been wanting for a long time. Big changes are built on small, almost invisible choices repeated over time.

WHY SMALL SHIFTS WORK FOR EXECUTIVE FUNCTION CHALLENGES

When executive functioning is already under strain, "go big or go home" often backfires. Small shifts work because they are:

- **Less Intimidating:** Your brain can start without the heavy lift of motivation or elaborate preparation
- **Low-Cost Experiments:** You can try something without fear of failing or wasting effort
- **Cumulative in Effect:** Small improvements

stack faster than you expect
- **Protective Against Burnout:** You avoid the "crash and burn" cycles that come from unsustainable overhauls

Example: I used to set my alarm an hour earlier to start a "perfect" morning routine. Within days, I would crash and sleep through the alarm. Switching to waking up just 10 minutes earlier for a stretch and coffee stuck for months and ended up being far more impactful than any perfect routine I had designed.

The compound effect is real. Walking one extra block on your daily route may not seem like much. But over a month, that is 30 extra blocks. Over a year, it is miles you would not have walked otherwise. Habits quietly build strength, stamina, and confidence.

EXAMPLES OF SMALL SHIFTS WITH BIG PAYOFF

These are not grand gestures. They are friction removers:

- Moving your medication next to the coffee pot so you do not forget it
- Putting your keys in a bright dish by the door
- Standing up to stretch every time you hit "send" on an email
- Asking one clarifying question at the start of a meeting to prevent hours of confusion later

Example: My to-do list used to live in a closed note-book. Out of sight meant out of mind. I moved it to a bright sticky note on my desk, and suddenly I did not "forget" my top priorities halfway through the day.

How to Identify Your Next Small Shift
Start by asking: "What feels hard right now?"

1. Find the friction point—the specific moment where the process breaks down.
2. Ask: "What is one tiny thing that would make it easier?"
3. Apply the rule: Make it visible. Make it obvious. Make it easier.

Example: I kept missing due dates for library books, even with reminders on my calendar. The fix was putting the books in front of the door the night before. It took less than a minute and saved a lot of frustration.

Building on the Win Without Overloading Yourself
Small shifts are tempting to stack. Once something works, your brain may want to pile on more changes. Resist that urge and try:

- Holding steady until the habit is truly automatic
- Celebrating before adding another change
- Protecting the win instead of risking it with too much too soon

Example: After I got in the habit of drinking a glass of water every morning, I wanted to add a workout, journaling, and meal prep right away. Instead, I kept the water habit steady for a month before adding something new. It lasted.

ENCOURAGEMENT AND ACCEPTANCE

You do not have to earn your progress by making it difficult.

Small wins are valid. They are proof you are moving forward, even if no one else sees them.

Self-talk swap: *Instead of "It is nothing," say "It is the start of something."*

Example: Sending one overdue email may not seem like much, but it can break the mental logjam and open the door for the next step. Small does not mean insignificant. It means sustainable.

When small feels too small, remember: if you have ever worn the wrong shoes on a walk, you know how something tiny can change the entire experience, for better or worse.

CLOSING GROUNDING TRUTH

You do not have to turn your life upside down to move it forward. The smallest hinge can swing the biggest door. Every small choice you make to reduce friction is a quiet investment in your future self. And each one builds a little more confidence that you can keep going.

WHY THIS MATTERS FOR NEURODIVERGENT BRAINS

Neurodivergent brains often face friction at the

starting line of tasks. By focusing on small, sustainable changes, you lower the mental load, strengthen follow-through, and build confidence without overwhelming your executive functioning skills.

 KEY TAKEAWAYS

Core Idea: Small shifts remove friction, lower the barrier to starting, and build momentum over time.

Big Shift: Do not underestimate tiny changes. They are the building blocks of lasting progress.

Practical Application: Identify one friction point in your day, make it easier by one step, and give it space to stick before adding anything new.

PUT IT INTO PRACTICE

Self-Talk: *One small thing is still a step forward.*

One Small Action for Future You: Pick one stalled task or habit and shrink it to a micro-action you can do today.

Reflection: If you made one tiny, almost invisible change today, what is the first ripple effect you would hope to see tomorrow?

You Don't Need to Be Fixed, You Need to Be Supported

Wrapping it up with self-trust, community, and hope

A client once told me, "I thought I was lazy until I learned my brain just worked differently. Now I ask for what I need instead of apologizing for who I am."

For years, they'd been told to "try harder," "be more disciplined," and "just get organized." Those words didn't make them better. They made them smaller. It wasn't until they understood their brain, found the right supports, and gave themselves permission to stop chasing perfection that things began to click.

We've been told our whole lives to "fix" ourselves. What we actually need is the right mix of supports, self-trust, and community to function as ourselves without apology.

WHY THE FIX-IT MINDSET FAILS

The "fix-it" mindset promises improvement but delivers

shame. It keeps you focused on everything you aren't instead of noticing what's already working. It:

- Creates shame, which fuels avoidance and burnout
- Reinforces the idea that there's a single "correct" way to live or work
- Tricks you into measuring progress against someone else's yardstick instead of your own values and needs

You can't build a sustainable life on self-criticism. The more energy you spend trying to be someone else's version of "enough," the less you have for what actually matters to you.

What True Support Looks Like

Support isn't about lowering the bar. It's about removing unnecessary barriers so you can show up for the things you care about.

It might look like:

- External tools that fit your brain, not someone else's perfect system
- People who believe you the first time you share your needs
- Environments that reduce friction and make starting easier
- Rhythms and routines that match your energy patterns, not the other way around

One client realized that moving their most-used work supplies into a rolling cart next to their desk saved them from breaking focus multiple times a day. They had been losing hours each week simply because key items were in another room. That small shift didn't just save time. it lowered frustration and made starting work feel less like an uphill climb.

BUILDING SELF-TRUST THROUGH SMALL EXPERIMENTS

You've seen this idea throughout the book: small shifts, not grand overhauls, are what build lasting self-trust.

Keep an experimental mindset. Nothing has to work forever to be worth trying now.

Track what's helping, not just what's hard, and treat repair and restarts as proof you keep showing up, not proof you failed.

In a previous chapter, you learned that micro-decisions, like moving your to-do list into plain sight, can ripple out in ways that change entire days. Every time you adapt instead of giving up, you strengthen the belief that you can figure things out again tomorrow.

ASKING FOR WHAT YOU NEED

One of the most powerful forms of self-support is the willingness to ask for it out loud. For example:

- "Could we agree on flexible deadlines when the project scope changes?"
- "Would you be willing to provide visual

instructions along with verbal ones?"
- "I'd like to set a consistent family routine for weekday mornings so we all start the day with less stress."

You don't need to justify your needs. You need to name them clearly and give others the chance to meet you there. Asking is not a weakness. It's a sign you're taking yourself seriously.

ACCEPTANCE AS AN ONGOING PRACTICE

Acceptance doesn't mean giving up. It means ending the constant battle with yourself long enough to build something that actually works.

Some days will still be messy. Some systems will break. That doesn't erase the progress you've made; it simply means you're human.

Self-talk swap: Instead of: "Why can't I just…" try: "What support would make this easier today?"

Think back to the chapters on boundaries, energy management, and mental flexibility. Those tools weren't meant to make you flawless. They were meant to make your life more livable in the reality you're already in.

A CALL-BACK TO WHERE YOU'VE BEEN

Over the last chapters, you've:

- Learned that small shifts can carry more

weight than giant overhauls
- Discovered that progress over perfection is more than a mindset; it's a strategy
- Practiced noticing when things are working so you can do more of them
- Seen how self-awareness, boundaries, and environment design work together to reduce friction
- Built confidence through experiments, not perfection

These aren't random tips. They're the framework for a life that supports you instead of drains you.

WHY THIS MATTERS FOR NEURODIVERGENT BRAINS

When your executive functioning is taxed, constant self-fixing talk only drains more energy. Supportive systems, environments, and relationships free up cognitive resources so you can focus on what matters, not on compensating for environments working against you.

CLOSING REFLECTION: YOUR SUPPORT MAP

Identify 3 things that support you today.

These can be tools, routines, people, or environments. For example:

- My daily planning
- My Wednesday co-working call
- Putting my phone in another room when I'm on a deadline

Note how each one helps. Why does it work? Does it lower overwhelm, boost focus, or make a task easier to start?

Choose one new support to try next week. Keep it small, something you can set up in less than 10 minutes. Commit to noticing.

At the end of the week, jot down when your supports helped and what difference they made.

Closing Grounding Truth

With the right supports, you can focus on what matters most and move through your days with less resistance. You don't have to do it alone.

 # KEY TAKEAWAYS

Core Idea: You don't need to be "fixed." You need supports, environments, and people that help you function as yourself.

Big Shift: Stop chasing a mythical version of yourself that needs no help, and start building a support map that reflects how your brain actually works.

Practical Application: Identify 3 supports you already have, note how they help, and choose one new micro-support to add this week.

🎯 PUT IT INTO PRACTICE

Self-Talk: *I don't have to be fixed. I just need the right supports.*

One Small Action for Future You: Identify one friction point in your day and remove a single barrier to make it easier.

Reflection: If you stopped trying to "fix" yourself and started focusing only on support, what would be the first thing you'd change?

Conclusion: A Note to You

If you've read this far, it means you care enough about your success to keep showing up for it. And that's no small thing.

You've already done more than you realize. You've identified friction points, swapped unhelpful self-talk for supportive language, and tested small changes to see what sticks. You've proven you can experiment, adapt, and restart without giving up.

This book is full of tools, frameworks, and reflections, but you don't need all of them at once. Some chapters will speak to you now, others later. The glossary at the back is there to ground you if the language ever feels new or overwhelming. Think of this book as a toolkit you can return to, not a checklist you have to complete.

I hope you close these pages knowing you have nothing to prove to earn the life you want. Every tiny choice you make in the direction of support, every micro-decision to rest, every boundary set, every system you adapt to fit your brain, is progress.

If you ever find yourself slipping back into shame or

overwhelm, flip to any chapter and pick one small step. You don't need the whole book in that moment; one reminder is enough to restart.

May you keep choosing the small, kind steps that add up to a life that feels like it belongs to you. And may you remember, always, that you've had what it takes from the start. You've been resourceful all along.

Glossary

This glossary is here to make the language in this book easier to follow. Think of it as a quick reference you can flip to whenever you want clarity. These are not clinical definitions. They are practical explanations, written for real life.

Accumulation Over Consistency: The idea that bursts of effort still add up over time, even if they do not happen every day or in the same way.

All-or-Nothing Thinking: A rigid mindset that sees only 2 options, success or failure, perfect or worthless, without recognizing the value of middle ground or partial progress.

Avoidance-Urgency Cycle: A loop where tasks are delayed until the last minute, then completed in a stressful rush of adrenaline. It works temporarily but often leads to exhaustion and guilt.

Crossing the Finish Line: A practice of valuing closure and completion more than perfection, because finishing something, even imperfectly, creates momentum and relief.

Emotional Labor: The effort of managing emotions, both your own and others, to keep interactions smooth and relationships steady.

Emotional Regulation: Managing feelings and reactions, especially in stressful or overwhelming situations, so you can respond instead of just react.

Energy Management: Paying attention to fuel, rest, and natural rhythms of energy throughout the day or week, and matching tasks to those rhythms rather than forcing productivity through willpower.

Executive Functioning (EF): A set of brain-based skills that help you plan, prioritize, start tasks, stay focused, regulate emotions, and follow through.

Future You: The version of yourself who benefits when you make supportive choices now, like laying out clothes the night before or paying a bill early.

Invisible Labor: The behind-the-scenes mental work of life, planning, anticipating, remembering, and coordinating tasks that others may not see but still take energy.

Mental Flexibility: The ability to shift perspectives, adjust plans, or see multiple solutions when things change.

Mono-Tasking: Doing one thing at a time with full attention, instead of splitting focus across multiple tasks.

Neurodivergent: A term describing people whose brains process, learn, or behave differently from what is considered typical.

Neurodiversity: The concept that brain differences are natural and valuable variations in human cognition.

Organization: Creating systems to keep track of tasks, plans, and important information in ways that reduce friction.

Planning: Looking ahead, breaking tasks into steps, and preparing for what is coming instead of only reacting in the moment.

Prioritizing: Choosing what comes first when everything feels urgent, and letting go of the idea that all tasks carry equal weight.

Process vs. Outcome Practices: Shifting focus from end results to actions within your control, which builds momentum and self-trust.

Productivity Guilt: The shame or self-criticism that comes from not meeting unrealistic expectations of constant productivity, even when rest or slower pro-gress is valid and necessary.

Rupture and Repair: A framework for recognizing when systems break down and practicing how to restart without shame.

State Story Strategy: A framework for understanding challenges, notice your current state (emotional, physical, mental), recognize the story you are telling yourself, and then choose a strategy that fits.

Task Initiation: The ability to begin tasks without excessive procrastination or avoidance.

Time Management: Using time wisely, estimating how long tasks take, and building systems that make deadlines visible and manageable.

Transition Menu: A personalized list of small practices like stretching, changing environments, or breathing that help ease the shift between tasks or roles.

Twice Exceptional (2e): A term for individuals who have both exceptional strengths, such as creativity or intelligence, and challenges, such as ADHD, dyslexia, or other learning differences.

Working Memory: The brain's ability to hold onto information just long enough to use it, such as remembering a phone number long enough to dial it or keeping the steps of a recipe in mind while cooking.

About the Author

Suzy Carbrey is a licensed speech-language pathologist turned ADHD and executive functioning coach who helps parents and professionals create lives that feel lighter, kinder, and more doable. Drawing on her clinical background and years of coaching experience, Suzy blends brain-based knowledge with practical strategies that actually work in real life. She lives near Chicago with her family, cats, and ever-growing garden.